NEW
DESIGN
IN CROCHET

Costumes, Bonnie Meltzer, mixed media. Imaginative costumes for a children's theater are reminiscent of Northwest Coast Indian dance regalia. (Photo by Bob Ellis)

NEW
DESIGN
IN CROCHET

Clinton D. MacKenzie

 VAN NOSTRAND REINHOLD COMPANY
New York Cincinnati Toronto London Melbourne

To Walter Nottingham,
who introduced me to the art of crochet,
and to my wife and daughter,
who stuck by me while I wrote the book

Acknowledgments

My special thanks to Sharyn Mills for the
exhaustive work on the line drawings for
this book

My gratitude to the following for their
assistance:

Mr. and Mrs. Oscar Brown, Mr. and Mrs.
Robert Burningham, Clifford Chieffo, Mary
Ann Glantz, Howard Gunderson, Tom
Hampton, Virginia Harvey, Linda Kramer,
Mrs. Malcolm Lein, Joan Lintault, Mr. and
Mrs. Robert McKenzie, Jim Morphesis, Robert
Mills, Nancy C. Newman, Jerry Samuelson,
Judith Vanderwall

And my students at California State
University, Fullerton, and Tyler School of Art

Van Nostrand Reinhold Company Regional Offices:
New York Cincinnati Chicago Millbrae Dallas
Van Nostrand Reinhold Company International Offices:
London Toronto Melbourne
Copyright © 1972 by Litton Educational Educational Publishing, Inc.
Library of Congress Catalog Card Number 72-1437
ISBN 0 442 350694
Designed by Visuality
Printed by Halliday Lithographic Corporation, Inc.
Color printed by Princeton Polychrome Corp.
Bound by The Book Press
Published by Van Nostrand Reinhold Company
A Division of Litton Educational Publishing, Inc.
450 West 33rd Street, New York, N.Y. 10001
Published simultaneously in Canada by
Van Nostrand Reinhold Ltd.
16   15   14   13   12   11   10   9   8   7   6   5   4   3   2   1

TOOLS COURTESY OF BOYE NEEDLE COMPANY, HERO MANUFACTURING COMPANY, AND SCOVILLE MANUFACTURING COMPANY

CONTENTS

INTRODUCTION

Wall Hanging No. 60, Isolde Savage, 70 inches, jute twine. A low-relief effect is created by joining strips of crochet that were made in different directions and adding tubular modules and lengths of single chains. (Photo by Lavers)

This book is based on principle rather than pattern. It is designed to allow more flexibility within the techniques of crochet than is allowed by previous, more traditional approaches, which stress only the making of domestic fabrics and wearing apparel such as afghans and booties. Crochet also can be a medium for pure artistic expression, as in wall hangings and sculptures, or can become a very personal art form through the making of jewelry, garments, and unique body ornaments.

Although this book emphasizes the "art fabric," I hope it will also serve as a guide for crocheters of utilitarian objects who work from patterns. The approach is flexible enough to be an inspiration to the hobbyist as well as to the creative artist, who needs only techniques and skill, rather than printed directions, to make his ideas tangible.

There are no pat answers here, and some of you may find that frustrating. All the elements necessary to create artworks from crochet are here, but the large responsibility—and freedom—of combining those elements rests on your shoulders. Probably the most important instruction underlying this text is: Be willing to experiment and investigate all of the possibilities. This attitude should be a prerequisite for reading the book.

If you only crochet one piece, you'll never know if you like to crochet or not. You'll probably only know the frustrations. Experience will help you decide. Try a piece that is intentionally a sample, using different stitches and techniques. Be happy with it as a sample rather than trying to make a masterpiece your first time out. There is no need to invest in expensive apparatus to try the techniques in this book. A crochet hook and butcher's twine will do the job.

Although there are a few new techniques presented here, the majority of the methods are traditional. This book, however, takes another look at these traditional techniques with the hope of presenting a new perspective—a perspective that stresses the principle underlying the techniques. The examples of finished works are limited because following patterns has not been emphasized. This is a new teaching direction that is only beginning to be explored.

A good deal of effort has been put into the instructional aspect of this book to make it the clearest and most easily understandable approach to crochet, using no abbreviations or shortcuts (although there is a reference list of commonly used abbreviations at the back of the book). At first glance, the experienced crocheter might think some of the information has been presented out of order. I have tried to present the techniques in the easiest order for learning. For example, the explanation of the slip stitch, which may seem logically to come first, has been placed after several other stitches simply because it is more difficult to manipulate.

A concerted effort has been made in the illustrations to represent the stitches exactly as they look while being made, so you will have a basis for comparison between your work and the drawings.

It is important for you to know that various books name stitches differently. In this book an attempt has been made to name the stitches graphically, with a term that describes something very basic about the stitch. The American system of naming crochet stitches is different from the British system: the British system names the stitches one step higher. A chart at the back of the book compares the two systems. For example, the American *single crochet* is what the English call a *double crochet.*

Crochet is a vital part of today's renaissance in the textile arts. You will see that there is room for crochet as a serious art form as well as a medium for hobbyists. Crochet is at best a technique from which the art object is made, and all that is presented here is not nearly so important as what you do with it after you have learned it. Crochet is merely a means to the art you make with it. The object will only be as good as the concept, not as good as the technique. If you want to make functional objects with these techniques, I hope that the functionalism will be secondary to aesthetics.

With crochet one can be as systematic as an architect assembling planes and as free as a poet describing his train of thought. Size and design possibilities are limited only by one's imagination and energies.

Enjoy!

Christian Symbol, Lissa Muench, 10 x 6
inches, wool

Fragment I, Clinton D. MacKenzie, 18 x 24
inches, natural raffia

Wall Hanging, Richard Daehnert, woven and crocheted wool

Ritual Vessel, Joan Sterrenburg, 25 x 15 inches, polytwine, silk, feathers (photo by artist)

Red Fantasy (Fancy), Clinton D. MacKenzie,
102 x 24 inches, wool and metallic fiber

Green Knight, Walter Nottingham, 108 x
30 inches, woven and crocheted wool,
linen, and synthetic fiber

Mask and Mantle, Heather McPherson,
12 x 60 inches, woven and crocheted raffia
with feathers

Celibacy, Walter Nottingham, 108 x 36
inches, woven and crocheted wool. Collection Museum of Modern Art, New York

Shawl, Carolyn Sotelo, 6 x 3 foot triangle, wool

Neckpiece, Arline Fisch, crocheted silver and gold wire

Wall Hanging, Charlene Burningham, 9 x 3½ feet, crocheted and woven wool and synthetics with beads, feathers, and bells

Mask, Heather McPherson, 15 inches high, linen (photo by artist)

Stoned, Bonnie Meltzer, life-size, jute (photo by artist)

Bound Figure, Barbara Shawcroft, 6 inches high, waxed linen

15

Red Vessel, Barbara Shawcroft, 11 inches
high, cotton roving and horsehair

Wall Hanging, Carole Beadle, 26 x 18
inches, wool and assorted yarns

1. HISTORY

The term "crochet" is derived from the French word *crocher* meaning to hook or to pick. France played the key role in the history of European lacemaking. The lacemaking terms most commonly used today all have French names, therefore the lace made with a hook became crochet.

The history of crochet is very difficult to trace because little is written about it and what is recorded comes in bits and pieces with many unexplained gaps. Probably, the gaps in the historical information are the result of various times when crochet was very obscure. But even when it was very popular, crochet instructions were not written but rather handed down from generation to generation. This section, therefore, includes some speculation and guesswork.

The earliest records of crochet come from South America along with information about other pre-Columbian textiles. A small group of primitive tribes used crocheted dress or ornaments in their puberty rites. The fabrics, which were probably made by the women of the tribes, were used in decorative bands or borders for the arms, ankles, and calves. In her book on knitting, Mary Thomas suggests that most South Americans did not use crochet until the Spanish brought it, the evidence for the cultural link being a similarity in the handmade hooks. She also states that, "knitting like other of its kindred arts [implying crochet] came from the East, from the Arabian peninsula from whence it spread eastward to Tibet, westward as far as Spain, carried thence to other Mediterranean ports by the Arabs who were the great traders of those days." She mentions that there are "knitting discoveries" dating from the fourth and fifth centuries in Coptic Egypt.

The tools used in the early days were like knitting needles with a small hook at one end. They were made of copper wire, iron, wood, bamboo, bone, ivory, and amber. Finger-crocheted braids and cords have also been found in ancient cultures.

Very often Soumak weaving is mistaken for crochet. Without taking the

Crocheted antimacassars, circa 1935, 4 x 15½ inches each, cotton. Collection of Mr. and Mrs. O. E. Brown. Heavy yarn changes the pattern proportions on designs earlier used in lacework.

fabric apart, you might mistake it for slip-stitching. One method of Soumak found in ancient fabrics is made by actually chaining the weft of a woven fabric. It is suspected that when weavers made the Soumak they used a type of crochet hook to form the wraps or chains on their warp.

It is interesting to note that crochet in its early stages seems to have been decorative rather than functional. Throughout its European history, crochet was referred to only as a type of lace. From the thirteenth through the sixteenth century crochet became known as "nun's work" because it was most commonly used by nuns to make altar linens and vestments. Many nuns still crochet their linens today. Crochet may well have spread to other countries with missionary nuns, as did many of the lace arts.

It ís likely but not certain that modern crochet was born from the tambour lace and hook found throughout Europe during the Renaissance. Tambour lace is embroidered on a machine-made mesh or netting background with a hook similar to our modern-day crochet hook. The hook is used to draw loops of linen through the mesh background. A stitch similar to a chain stitch in crocheting is made when the loops are drawn through the mesh and through one another. We can speculate that at one point the mesh background was dropped and the crochet hook became independent, being used to make a series of chains that formed a fabric free from the machine-made groundwork. It is likely that crochet and tambour lace were at one time worked side-by-side, and ultimately the speed and definition of the crochet won favor. Crocheted lace became an art form relished by kings and queens. They wore edgings and fringes and decorated their drawing rooms with crochet.

Particularly in the development of European crocheted laces, the men as well as the women played an important part. Men designed and made crocheted lace, and boys as well as girls were taught lacemaking in school.

In the total spectrum of European lacemaking, crochet has only played a minor role except in the country of Ireland, where the Irish used it to imitate the very popular and expensive Venetian laces. Crochet helped to save Ireland's economy after the great famine of the nineteenth century. Home or cottage in-

dustries in crochet were started because everyone could afford to make his own small crochet hook and to buy linen or spin his own. This new kind of lacemaking was so successful a venture that it helped to save the country from ruin.

Irish lace, which did not originate in Ireland, since it was also being made in Italy and other parts of Southern Europe, is characterized by figures such as flowers, leaves, and birds. These motifs are crocheted separately and joined together with a crocheted mesh ground. The visual firmness of the motif is attained by cro-

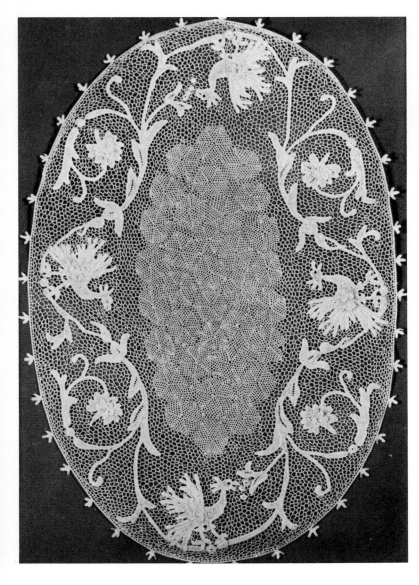

Irish lace, circa 1850, 11 x 17 inches, cotton. Courtesy Minnesota Museum of Art, Allwardt Collection. Irish lace is characterized by motifs, such as birds and flowers, that have been joined together with a crocheted mesh background.

Irish lace cuffs, 19th century, 9 x 3⅜ inches each, cotton. Courtesy Minnesota Museum of Art, Barnwell Collection. Crocheted cuffs were worn by the nobility in Europe in the 18th and 19th centuries.

cheting over a soft cotton padding cord instead of the usual crocheted chain. There are many variations to the mesh background, but the fanciest have small picots on the chain links that make up the net ground. The effects achieved when the motifs are combined with the background are very intricate and completely unique.

Throughout Europe and then throughout America, crochet was often used for borders and edgings on woven fabrics. Typically, collars, cuffs, and hems were made of crochet. Later, decorative interior fabrics were used for table coverings and furniture embellishments.

The twentieth century has seen crochet being used in new ways. In the 1940s in America crochet became very popular for making ornamental trimmings of light threads, such as doilies, which were commonly found in every home. Heavy yarns were introduced for making bedspreads and chair backs. Cro-

cheted wearing apparel similar to knitted garments began to appear in the 1950s. The usual items were hats, afghans, shawls, and baby clothing, and they were made from wool, cotton, and some of the then new synthetics. In the late 1960s, a few artists in the United States began to use crochet as a vehicle for an art fabric or as an art form. Men are taking a major role alongside women in this movement that takes crochet out of a realm limited merely to fashion and household items.

The use of much larger tools and yarns and the application of new materials are but a few of the major differences to take place between traditional and contemporary crochet. We have expanded the art to meet new needs and design considerations. Artists have come to recognize and employ crochet's most unique characteristics and inherent properties, and many examples throughout the book illustrate this new sensitivity.

Crocheted handbag, circa 1910, 7 x 12 inches, cotton. Collection of Mr. and Mrs. O. E. Brown. An open network of arc stitches is complemented by a raised rosette.

Crocheted doily, circa 1935, 14 inches in diameter. Collection of Mr. and Mrs. O. E. Brown. This pineapple pattern was commonly seen on doilies in American homes of the 1940s.

2. TOOLS

Very few tools are needed for crochet, unlike many other textile techniques. A crochet hook, or perhaps a selection of hooks, and yarn or cord are the basics. Experimenting with two or three different sizes of hook will disclose the different effects that each has on the fabric construction, and using more than one size

hook in the same piece will create varied effects, as will working with two or three yarns or cords of different diameters and fibers. One small hook is also good for working in ends.

In addition to your hooks, you need a pair of scissors, and a cloth or plastic measuring tape and markers are often

Tools necessary for crocheting: *(left to right)* scissors, pins, selection of hooks, yarn needles, paper clips or other markers, measuring tape, and gauge (at bottom).

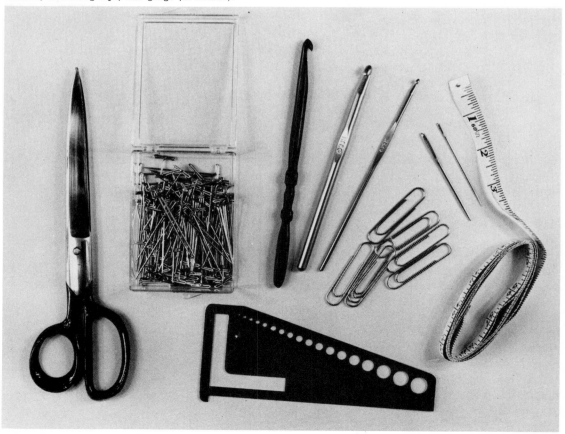

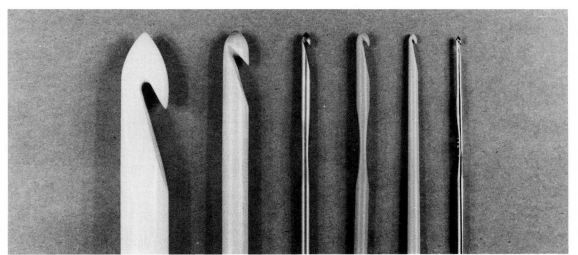

2-1. Crochet hooks are made from many different materials including *(left to right)* casein, wood, aluminum, plastic, bone, and steel

helpful. Makeshift markers such as safety pins, paper clips, or colored yarn will work as well as commercially made markers. A tapestry or yarn needle can be used for working in ends, splicing yarns, and sewing pieces together. Pins are also helpful for temporarily marking pieces or fitting them together. A large handbag or book bag to carry your crochet in is a good investment.

All of the supplies, tools, and materials needed to begin crochet can be bought at most variety and department stores. When you are purchasing tools, buy the best, since even the best tools are inexpensive. Unless you are careless a good hook will last a lifetime, and you can break it in yourself, like a favorite pen.

Look for a hook which is lightweight, easy to handle, and comfortable. It should have a finely ground head that is deeply cut to grasp the yarn easily. Crochet hooks are made from many different materials including steel, aluminum, plastic, wood, and casein (Fig. 2-1). The finer or smaller hooks, generally less than ¼″ in diameter and only 5″ long, are made from steel because steel can be drawn very fine and remain strong. Aluminum and plastic are used for larger sizes

because of their light weight and strength. Very large hooks are usually made from wood, plastic, or casein because these materials, too, are light and inexpensive.

Most regular crochet hooks have three main parts. The shank or shaft of the hook determines the size of each stitch. The hook at the end is used to catch the yarn to make the loops while crocheting. On metal and plastic hooks there is usually a depression or flattened area on the shank which merely makes the crochet hook easy to grip. Wooden or casein hooks rarely have this indentation since they are quite large and therefore easy to hold.

Afghan or tunisian hooks are quite different from the regular crochet hooks. They are made to hold a complete row of stitches as you work, as in knitting. They have straight, even shafts and look like knitting needles with a crochet hook at one end and a metal or plastic tip at the other. A new variation of the afghan hook has been developed with a flexible cable shaft.

Making your own tools, fashioned for your particular needs, is possible and often desirable. Nontraditional uses of crochet may call for special tools to fit needs previously unthought of, and an afternoon spent carving a special crochet hook may save hours of labor.

Finger crochet, in which the index finger is used as the hook, is still another approach. There are no tools as handy or as versatile as your fingers. The basic stitches are easily manipulated with your hands. The direct handling of materials creates an internal communication that makes you feel closer to your work and more a part of the finished product. This may be reason enough to create whole pieces just using finger crochet, but the technique also may help a beginner overcome the initial clumsiness of handling the hook. Problem situations may arise in which finger crochet will serve as the best or the only solution.

The sizing of hooks is rather confusing because several systems are employed. To help you in purchasing hooks, the information about hook sizes and materials that follows is summarized in a chart at the back of the book. There are some constants, however. Steel hooks are sized by number and the larger the number, the finer the hook is. The numbers on steel hooks range from number 14, which is the finest, to 2/0 or 00, which is the largest. Steel hooks are most commonly used for fine crochet cottons, linens, and lightweight yarns. For our contemporary yarns, the differences between steel needle sizes makes so little difference that you can often substitute the size you have for what the manufacturer recommends.

Aluminum hooks, the most popular, are made in sizes denoted by letters ranging from B through K. B is the smallest and K is the largest. There is some overlap in sizes between steel hooks and aluminum hooks. Size B aluminum corresponds roughly to size 2 steel, size C to size 0, and Size D to size 00. Aluminum hooks are primarily used for standard knitting yarns and heavier cords.

Plastic hooks are made in sizes denoted by numbers 1 through 10½ and also by letters D through K. The numerical system, however, is not standardized, and there may be variations in the sizes of numbered plastic hooks. To ease the confusion, there are also overlaps between aluminum and plastic hooks: sizes D through K are usually interchangeable with aluminum hooks of the same letter. On plastic hooks with numbers, according to a major manufacturer of hooks, the numbers relate to letters on plastic and aluminum hooks approximately as follows: 3 equals D, 4 equals E, 5 equals F, 6 equals G, 7 has no counterpart, 8 equals H, 9 equals I, 10 equals J, and 10½ equals K. Plastic hooks are generally used with softer knitting yarns and lightweight work, since they are flexible. You must learn to work lightly with plastic hooks to avoid breaking them.

Bone hooks have a tapered shaft and have their own size system. They are numbered 1 through 6. Number 1 is the smallest and is roughly equivalent to size B in aluminum; number 6 is the largest and is roughly equivalent to size F in aluminum or plastic. Bone is the traditional hook used for fine woolens and lightweight work. Like plastic hooks they will break unless you work lightly with them. Most of the "bone" type hooks sold today are made of plastic.

Wooden hooks are sized numerically, with numbers 10, 11, 13, 15, and 16. Number 10 is the smallest and 16 is the largest. Wooden hooks are very large and used for working very fast with rug yarns, heavy cords, or several strands of yarn. They are also used with lighter weight cords to create open, lacy effects.

Giant plastic or casein hooks come in two sizes, Q and S. These hooks are used primarily for bulky jobs. The easiest way to measure these oversize hooks is by diameter, and gauges for measuring crochet hooks and knitting needles are usually available from retailers of hooks.

The diameters of wooden hooks are, approximately: 10 equals ¼", 11 equals ⁵⁄₁₆" 13 equals ⅜", 15 equals ⁷⁄₁₆", and 16 equals ½". The diameters of plastic hooks sized Q are ⅝″ and sized S are ¾″.

The length of crochet hooks varies, too. Steel hooks are 5″ long, plastic hooks are 5½″ long, and aluminum hooks are 6″ long. Wooden hooks are usually 9″ or 10″ long, and the giant plastic hooks are about 8″ long.

Afghan hooks, mostly made of aluminum, are the longest of all—9″ to 14″. They are sized both by number and by letter. Numbers 1 through 10 correspond roughly to the same size in knitting needles. Afghan hooks sized by letter, B through J, are roughly equivalent to aluminum or plastic crochet hooks of the same letter.

The right size hook is the one that handles the yarn easily. You must be able to catch the yarn without splitting it or snagging in the work. Hook sizes and materials are summarized in a chart at the back of the book.

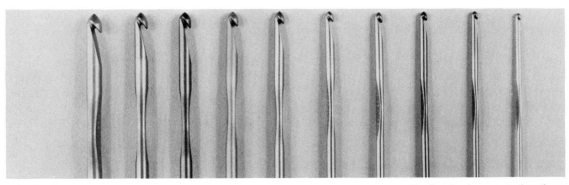

Aluminum hooks are the most popular, and range from size B (the smallest) to size K (the largest).

Crochet hooks vary in length as well as in diameter. The long afghan hook, 9 to 14 inches; wooden hook, 9 to 10 inches; giant plastic hook, 8 inches; aluminum hook, 6 inches; plastic hook, 5½ inches; steel hook, 5 inches.

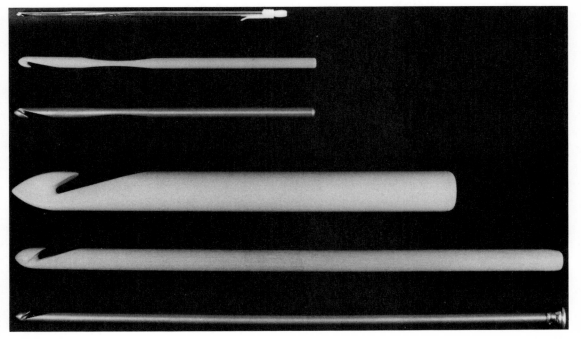

3. MATERIALS

One of the primary differences between traditional crochet and contemporary crochet is the much wider range of materials that have been used in the last twenty years. Traditional materials were very limited because the articles made were primarily domestic interior fabrics or fine apparel. Cotton and linen were employed regularly, and on special occasions silk was used. The yarns were also limited in color to white, cream, or ecru. There are cotton threads still available made specifically for household fabrics and to be used with specific steel hooks. Suppliers usually have charts for matching thread to hook.

Recently wool and synthetic fibers have been used extensively, but not until the

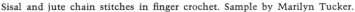

Sisal and jute chain stitches in finger crochet. Sample by Marilyn Tucker.

mid-1960s did crocheters throw away all customs and say that anything was possible. The ceiling was lifted, so to speak, on the selection of materials. For art fabric, any and all fibers are used, along with wire, plastic, leather, and whatever else might suit the particular artist's direction. Examples in this book include articles of crochet employing raffia, silver wire, plastic tubing, and many other materials.

Yarns and cords are available in a wide variety of sizes, spins, colors, and fibers. Natural fibers consist of plant and animal products including wool, silk, cotton, linen, jute, flax, manila, sisal, hemp, raffia, and paper (wood fiber). There are also many interesting man-made fibers, including rayon, nylon, Orlon, fiberglass, plastic, polyethylene, polypropylene, and others. There are also blends of the synthetic and natural fibers and novelty yarns, including metallic threads, ribbons, plastic straw, and yarns of unusual materials and spins. For making utilitarian items, washability, hand, and color fastness are all characteristics that should be taken into consideration when choosing materials.

Most cords or yarns are plied, meaning they are made of separate strands that have been twisted together. If the strands separate easily, the yarn will be harder to work with, especially for a beginning crocheter. (Of course, a hook large enough to grasp the whole cord easily will help

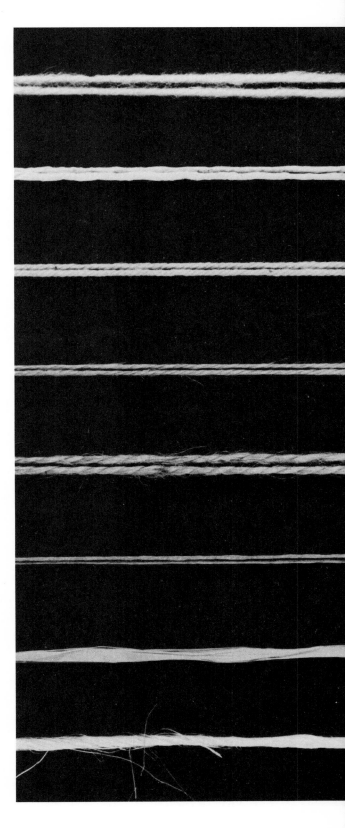

Natural materials for crochet *(top to bottom)*: wool, 10-ply cotton, cotton seine twine, linen rug warp, 2-ply jute, spun paper, natural raffia, sisal.

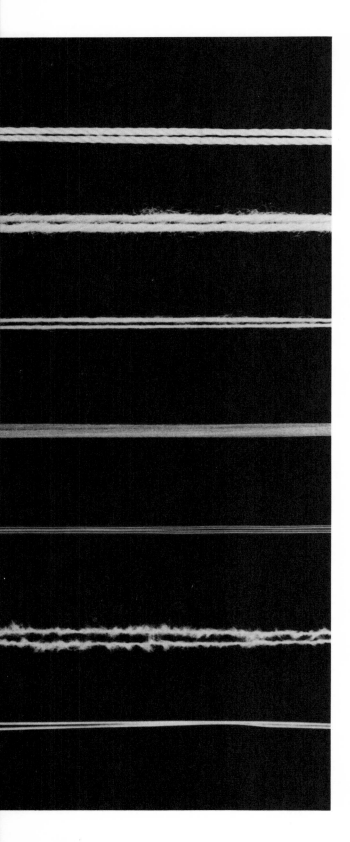

Synthetic materials for crochet *(top to bottom)*: nylon seine twine, wool-spun nylon, rayon, nylon roving, clear nylon monofilament, spun fiberglass, wire (annealed).

The following samples show the crocheted effect of different materials. Each sample has been made in single crochet with a size H hook.

Wool is stretchy and soft with a slightly coarse surface. It is suitable for garments and art fabric.

Ten-ply cotton string is soft and smooth-surfaced but not elastic.

prevent splitting of plied yarns.) Braided cords or monofilaments seldom split in this way. When you are learning to crochet, stay away from the more exotic materials such as wire and raffia, since they are more difficult to handle.

If you are going to spend a lot of time on a project, it is wise to buy good materials, and buying all of the yarn needed at once will avoid changes in dye lots or spinning. This is advisable if you are concerned about matching color or tex-

Cotton seine twine is stiff, nonelastic, and has a cabled surface. Its properties make it very suitable for rigid forms.

Linen rug warp is nonelastic but soft, and has a smooth surface.

ture exactly. With the recent upsurge in the textile arts, materials are generally available in a wide variety of colors. However, if a particular color you need is not available, don't be afraid to dye it yourself. There are household dyes available for this purpose that are simple to use, and there are professional studio and industrial dyes for the more experienced craftsman.

The quality of the material affects the construction of a crocheted fabric con-

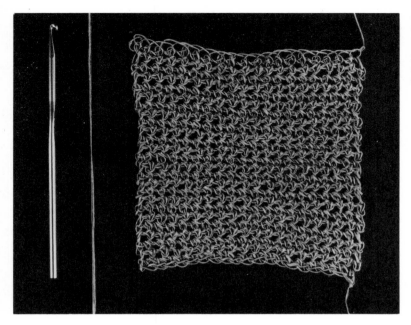

Spun paper cords are extremely stiff and have no elasticity, but their coarseness and unique look are often desirable in art fabrics. Because it is not washable, spun paper is a poor choice for garments.

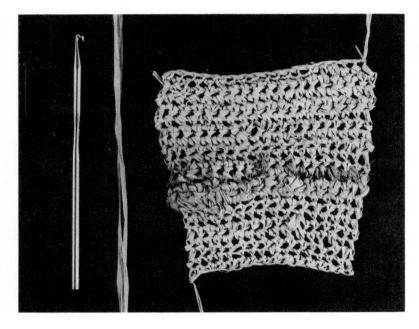

Natural raffia is stiff, nonelastic, and has an unmistakable, uneven texture. Its short lengths necessitate changing strands very often.

siderably. The body or firmness, rigidity, texture, and elasticity of the piece depend on the yarn. The elasticity of the yarn is a primary consideration. If you use an elastic fiber like wool for a hanging, the weight of the piece might pull it out of shape. When such stretch is an undesirable property, a nonelastic fiber such as linen or some synthetic would be more suitable.

A nonelastic yarn or cord may be the best to learn with. It will show any irreg-

Nylon seine twin is soft, smooth, and nonelastic. It makes a shiny, pliable fabric.

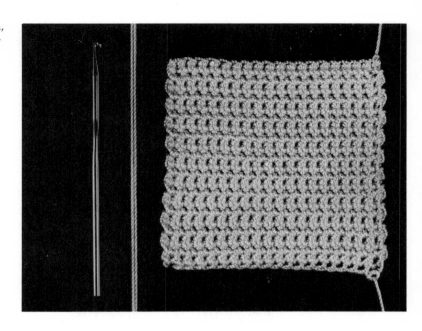

Wool-spun nylon is soft and nonelastic. Its fibrous surface nearly disguises the stitches.

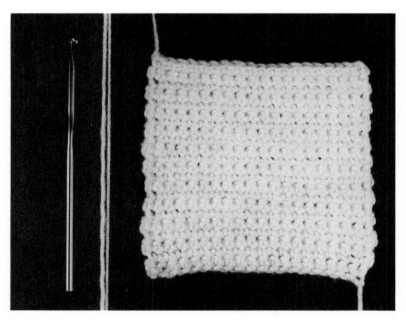

ularity in the stitches, therefore making it clear where to make adjustments. Bear in mind, however, that you will only gain consistency in your stitches with practice.

The stiffness of the yarn or fiber is another property to consider. Generally, softer yarns will make a more pliable fabric, and stiffer yarns will make a firmer or more rigid fabric. This is particularly important if any part of the work is to be made rigid enough to hold its own shape.

The selection of finish, or texture of

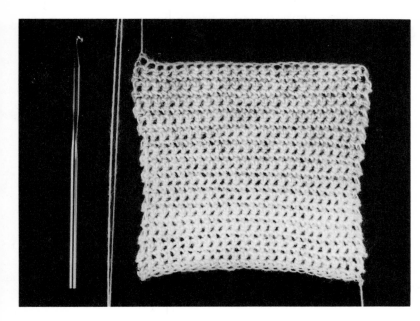

Rayon yarn is coarse, soft, and nonelastic. It holds the shape of each stitch very well.

spin, also affects pliability. Smoother or slicker fibers make a more pliable fabric than the coarser yarns. Yarn finish can also change the appearance of stitches. A smooth-surfaced fiber with a hard spin will show every aspect of each stitch, whereas a coarse, fibrous surface will disguise the stitches, often to the point of hiding the fact that the fabric is crocheted.

Gauge, in crochet, refers to the density of the stitches or to the size of the holes in the fabric, whichever you prefer. The size or diameter of the yarn relative to the size of the hook determines the density. Generally the principle applies that small or fine yarns used with large hooks create a less dense or more open fabric. Conversely, the larger the yarn and the smaller the hook, the more dense the fabric will be. There is a point, however, where the tool can be overloaded. This creates problems because the stitches must be forced, which may split the yarn unless it has a hard spin.

Gauge affects the body and rigidity of the fabric and also changes the texture and the elasticity. Gauge is usually important in making garments and interior fabrics, and where matching parts is of concern. In soft sculpture, the rigidity may be a very important factor, especially if the form is to be self-supporting.

In making wearing apparel or interior furnishings, the gauge is always given, along with the type of yarn and size of hook, with the pattern. Gauge is usually given in stitches per inch (5 sts. = 1"), rows (5 rows = 1") or rounds per inch (4 rnds. = 1"), or pattern rows (5 pattern rows = 6") or pattern repeats per inch (5 patterns = 3"). If you do not work from patterns and you intend to duplicate parts that you have made yourself, it is very important to keep notes on gauge.

When checking gauge, lay a tape meas-

To check gauge (find the number of stitches per inch), count the number of stitches between pins marking a two-inch length of fabric, and divide by two.

ure on the fabric and insert a pin at each end of a two-inch span. Count the stitches between the two pins and divide by two to find the number of stitches per inch. Often there will be half a stitch in question, and measuring two inches usually clarifies that point.

If after checking your gauge you decide to change density, there are two ways to do it. The relationship between the size of the yarn and the size of hook selected is the first to consider. If you have too many stitches, meaning that the work is too tight, you must move to a larger-sized hook. If you have too few stitches, or the work is too loose, select a smaller hook. If the gauge is correct in a large-scale piece of work but you want the work to be more rigid, use a slightly larger yarn or add another yarn in order to crochet with two yarns at once. Secondly, consider the tension on the yarn as you make the stitch. Tightening the yarn will make a denser, more rigid fabric with more stitches per inch. Easing up on the yarn will make a looser, more pliable fabric with fewer stitches per inch.

You must not think that materials can only be bought at yarn stores or department stores. Try a hardware store, cordage company, surplus store, variety store, craft supplier, knitting-yarn supplier, or weaving supplier. Once you are tuned in to looking for crochet materials, you will be surprised at the variety of places they turn up.

There are as many different ways of buying these materials as there are sources to buy them from. Some will be sold by measure of length, some by weight, some by the ball or cone. This depends upon the source and type of material.

There is no accurate way to calculate the amount of yarn or other materials you will need if you are not working from a pattern or a given set of instructions. The most effective method for estimating how much material you need is to make a sample with the actual yarn and hook chosen, to the gauge or density that you will ultimately make the piece. Then estimate the size of the finished piece and determine how much material was used in the small sample. From these figures you can determine how much yarn you will need. It is a good idea to retain the samples for future reference in a notebook, or with notes attached to the piece, to identify particular characteristics.

When you choose materials, if there is a question about whether something will work or not, it probably will. Anyway, try it. If you don't, you may never get started. Crochet can be incorporated with other materials such as ceramics, wood, leather, and metal. It can also become a medium for soft sculpture, using other fabrics and vinyls. Be adventurous.

When the same yarn is used with different hooks, the gauge of the fabric changes. The swatch that has more stitches per inch, that is, the one that looks tighter, was made with a size K hook. The looser swatch was made with a hook of larger diameter, size H.

Crocheted transparent plastic tape creates an unusual light-reflective surface. Sample by Laurie Warner.

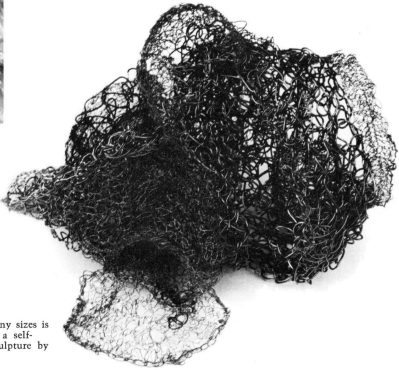

Copper wire of many sizes is crocheted to form a self-supporting wire sculpture by Elizabeth Bran.

4. BASIC STITCHES

Crochet is a single-element fabric construction employing a hook to do interlooping, meaning to draw a loop through a loop. It is worked in rows or rounds with a continuous strand. This gives the crocheter the advantage of not having to premeasure lengths of yarn as in weaving or macramé.

Crochet is not difficult to learn, but the coordination necessary for smooth working of the hook takes practice. At first it may seem as if you are working with your feet rather than your hands. Practice not only develops skill, but a personal rhythm.

There are several different types of

This detail of *Wall Hanging No. 60* by Isolde Savage shows how chains and very simple stitches can be used to artistic effect.

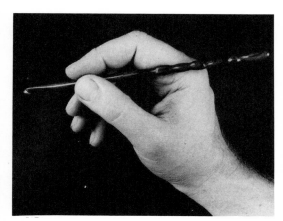

4-1. Traditional hold on a crochet hook

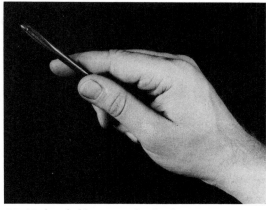

4-2. Modern hold on a crochet hook

crochet including basic crochet, filet crochet, Irish crochet, afghan crochet, and hairpin lace. The information in the following chapters deals with the most basic principles underlying all of the types. All of the crochet stitches, including the fanciest, are a variation or enlargement of one of the several basic stitches. Many pieces are simply done with one or a combination of single, double, or triple crochet. It is unnecessary to know fancy stitches to make a good piece. Rather than muster a lot of techniques, make a simple piece and push it to do something special. Start from a sketch or just let it flow. One of the special characteristics of crochet is the freedom to wander freely or plan your moves in advance.

Unlike knitting, crochet is easy to control as it grows because there is only one loop on the hook at the completion of each stitch.

Because each stitch is locked, or in effect knotted, crochet stitches will hold their shape. However, the softness of crochet is a desirable characteristic that can be fully utilized if it is considered before building it into a piece. The softness of art fabric is a decided advantage since the piece can usually be folded or collapsed for shipping, and it is very lightweight. Whoever heard of a ten-foot-high sculpture being shipped in a five-inch-high box? You can do just that with a sculptural crochet form.

Begin practicing with an easy-to-handle hook, size E to H. Watch while you work. Your hold on the hook and yarn and the positioning of your hands are very important to success with crochet. There are several ways to hold the crochet hook. The traditional way is similar to holding a pen (Fig. 4-1). With large hooks and heavy yarns, a grip similar to that used with an awl will give you more reserve strength (Fig. 4-2). However, contrary to most traditional prescriptions, holding the hook is a matter of comfort. Find the way that suits you best and try to relax; it will make learning to crochet much easier. As you launch into the technical information, bear in mind that any technical approach is justified as long as it achieves the desired end results.

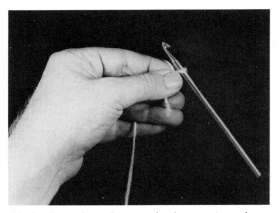

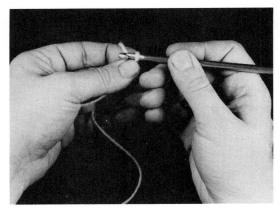

4-3. In the traditional approach, the yarn must be picked up from the top of the index finger

4-4. Traditionally, the index and second fingers adjust the flow of the supply yarn

There are also several ways to hold the yarn. The tension applied to the yarn is the most important part of holding the yarn. If the thread flows too freely, the stitches will usually become too large, and if held too tightly, the stitches will become too small and tight. Therefore, you must find a comfortable average. It is far more important that you have even tension than whether your tension is particularly loose or tight. Relax and your work will flow evenly.

In the traditional approach (Figs. 4-3 and 4-4), the yarn must be picked up from the top of the index finger, which is best done with a small hook. The path of the supply yarn through the index and second fingers becomes the lever for adjusting the flow. By squeezing the fingers lightly or letting them loose you can change the tension. With the second method, more suitable to working with today's larger hooks and materials, the supply yarn is picked up between the grasp on the stitches (between the thumb and third finger) and the index finger. (Figs. 4-5 and 4-6). The finger becomes a device to adjust the tension. If you have

not crocheted before, I would suggest the second method. This method gives a clear and distinct place from which to pick up the yarn, it makes tension adjustment easy, and leaves all of the work to be done by the hand holding the hook.

If you are right-handed, hold nothing but the hook in your right hand. Hold the yarn and the body of the fabric in the left hand, so that your right hand is completely free to manipulate the hook. The left hand essentially remains still, the work being done with the right hand. The reverse should be followed by the left-handed person.

Slip knot

A slip knot is used to start the chain that all regular crochet stitches begin with. A series of chain stitches make up the foundation chain or starting chain of any crochet piece. The slip knot is made by forming an arc with the yarn and twisting it (Fig. 4-7), after which the yarn coming from the yarn supply is pulled through the loop made by the twist (Fig. 4-8). Pull the yarn tight to complete the slip knot (Fig. 4-9).

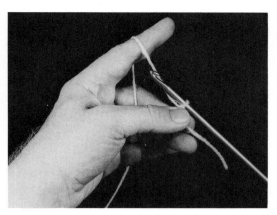 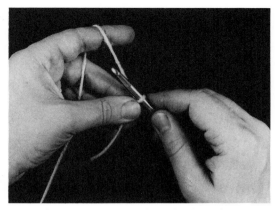

4-5. In the modern approach, the supply yarn is picked up between the grasp on the stitches (with the thumb and third finger) and the index finger

4-6. With this sturdier grip, the index finger becomes the device to adjust the tension

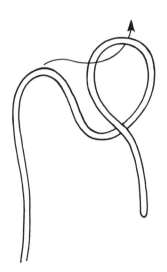 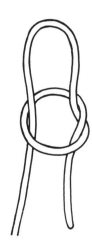 

4-7. Slip knot, step one

4-8. Slip knot, step two

4-9. Slip knot, step three

The yarn that feeds into the work from your supply is referred to as the source yarn. When making the slip knot it is possible to get this backwards so that when you pull on the cut end the loop over the hook will tighten up. This is incorrect. You have pulled the wrong string through the loop.

Insert the hook into the slip knot and draw the slip knot down onto the shank of the hook. You are now ready to begin crocheting.

Chain stitch

The chain stitch is the basic stitch that is compounded to make all other crochet stitches. To make the chain stitch, pass the hook to the left and under the yarn (Fig. 4-10), catch the yarn, and draw it through the loop on the hook, making a new loop or chain stitch. Repeat this stitch until the foundation chain is the desired length. At the beginning, your work will twist and curl. After the foundation chain is made, the addition of more rows will make the piece flatten out.

Catching the yarn to draw each stitch is simpler and will make your work easier than throwing the yarn, as done in the American system of knitting. Also, you must *always* pick up the yarn by passing the hook to the left and under the yarn, unless otherwise directed. Since you are in effect wrapping the yarn over the hook, this is often referred to as a "yarn over" or "wool round hook."

Each successive loop should slip through without taking muscle to do it. You should be able to draw the yarn through the loop using only your fingertips to grip the hook. As you draw the yarn through each loop, you must be careful not to close the loop by pulling the yarn from the source too tight. Once the yarn is caught, the tension can be relaxed as you bring it through the loop. Since the size of the stitch is determined by the shank of the hook, each loop must be slipped fully on to it and remain the same size as it is slipped off.

Your grip on the stitches can be moved closer to the hook as each stitch is completed, making it easier to get the hook through the stitch. It is also helpful to turn the hook as you draw it through the stitch so it comes through upside down. This prevents the hook from catching the loop you are drawing through.

When the chain is complete, notice that there are two sides or faces to it. One side is flat; the other has a ridge on it. When looking at the flat side, which we will call the front, note that it looks like loops are growing out of one another (Fig. 4-11). If you turn the chain over to

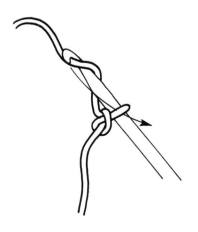

4-10. Chain stitch

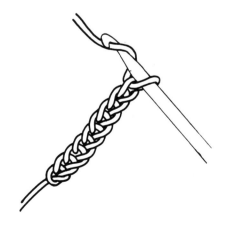

4-11. Foundation chain shown from the front

the back, or the side with the ridge, it looks like there is an attaching stitch sewn through each loop (Fig. 4-12). Whether specific directions suggest working from the front or the back, you must be careful not to twist the chain or it will spoil the edge of the fabric.

Counting stitches

The foundation chain forms the groundwork for each piece, so you should consider its length to be the length of the piece you are going to make. There will be about a 10 to 20 per cent take-up in the length of the chain as you make the second and third rows of the fabric. Beginners may want to make a sample with the actual materials to see how much take-up there will be, so that adjustments can be made accordingly.

If you are counting stitches, everything but the loop on the hook is counted. (As the yarn is caught and drawn through it, the slip knot at the beginning becomes a stitch.) The loop on the hook will become part of the next stitch made. When crochet is worked in rows, a certain number of chains must be added at the end of each row to bring the yarn or hook to the appropriate height for the next row. This also applies to the starting chain. When you crochet a particular length or given number of stitches, make the

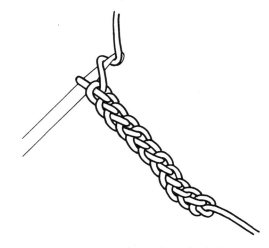

4-12. Foundation chain shown from the back

foundation chain one stitch longer to begin a row of single crochets, two for a half-double crochet, three for a double, etc. (See chart at end of this chapter.)

Non-ribbed and ribbed stitches

There are two variations of the single, double, and triple crochet stitches, one of which is ribbed and one which is not.

Ribbed single crochet

Nonribbed single crochet. This is the basic building block of many complicated crochet stitches.

Each variation depends on the number of threads picked up as you begin a stitch. Non-ribbed stitches, in which you pick up two threads, make a fabric with heavier body and less apparent surface delineation of the direction in which the crochet has been worked than the ribbed stitches, in which you pick up only one thread. Both the non-ribbed and ribbed stitch can be useful, depending on the surface texture or body you want. It is entirely possible and often desirable to use both kinds of stitches in the same piece.

Single crochet

To begin a row of either regular (non-ribbed) or ribbed single crochet stitches, start with a foundation chain. Working from the front of the chain, begin by inserting the hook from the front to the back into the *second chain* from the hook (Fig. 4-13). The seeming extra stitch will give you the proper height at the edge of your piece. Catch the yarn by passing the hook to the left of the yarn and under, and draw it through the chain stitch and onto the hook (Fig. 4-14), which leaves two loops on the hook. Catch the yarn again and pull it through both loops (Fig. 4-15). You have completed a single crochet stitch (Fig. 4-16). Insert the hook into the next chain stitch and repeat the instructions until you have completed the first row of single crochets. When you are working the first row on the foundation, the work will go slowly because it is difficult to hold.

When the last stitch has been made and you are ready to turn, add one chain stitch (Fig. 4-17) and turn the fabric around so you are looking at the back side, with the row of stitches just completed on top (Fig. 4-18). (The stitch at the end of a row of single crochet is added to allow enough yarn to turn, without diminishing the row by one stitch each time, thereby tapering the edges.) Insert the hook under the two top threads of the last complete stitch

4-13. Insert for single crochet

4-14. Single crochet, step one

4-15. Single crochet, step two

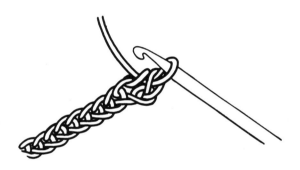

4-16. Single crochet, completed

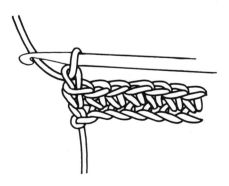

4-17. Turn for single crochet, step one

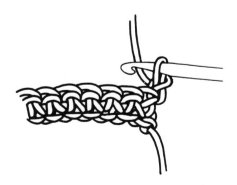

4-18. Turn for single crochet, step two

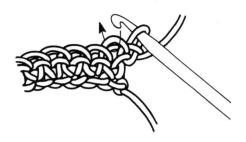

4-19. Picking up two threads in insert for single crochet

4-20. Picking up one thread in insert for single crochet

of the preceding row (Fig. 4-19). Work the second and succeeding rows of regular crochet using these same steps.

When making the first row of single crochets, hold the chain with the thumb and middle finger, as you had gripped the tail of the foundation chain, and let the new row of stitches fall free. If you are having difficulty getting the hook into the stitches in the previous row, it is probably because you have not carried each stitch onto the largest diameter of the hook, thus not leaving the proper amount of space to work back into.

Ribbed single crochet

The second variation of the single crochet, the ribbed stitch, is made with the same basic steps as the regular single crochet. The exception is that when the stitch is started in the second row, you pick up only one thread at the top of the stitch. As you turn the fabric to continue each successive row, pick up either of the two top threads (Fig. 4-20), instead of picking up both top threads as you do for the regular stitches (Fig. 4-19). If you pick up the front top thread (the one nearest you), it will make only a surface change. If you pick up the back top thread, you will get a rib in relief.

Double crochet

When moving from single crochet to double to triple, you are in effect increasing the height of each stitch. With this change comes a sacrifice of some firmness or body in the fabric. Double crochet is a faster way of working than single crochet, and triple is faster than double, but if you need a particular body or firmness in the fabric you must decide which stitch is the most efficient and still provides the most appropriate construction. Beside the selection of stitch, the firmness of construction varies with non-ribbed or ribbed stitches and with the relationship between the size of yarn and the size of the hook.

Double crochet is a stitch that is two

Double crochet

4-21. Insert for double crochet

rows high and made in a single passage. It is also started from a foundation chain. Begin the double crochet by wrapping the yarn around the hook once (passing the hook from the left and under) and inserting it from the front into the *fourth chain stitch* from the hook (Fig. 4-21).

4-22. Double crochet, step one

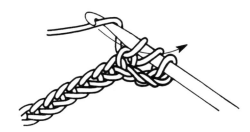

4-23. Double crochet, step two

4-24. Double crochet, step three

4-25. Double crochet, completed

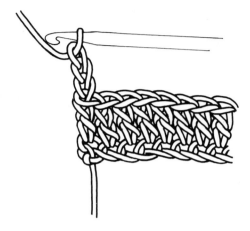

4-26. Turn for double crochet, step one

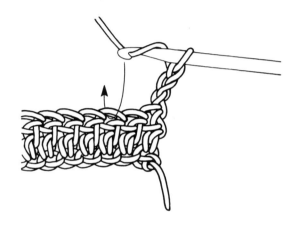

4-27. Turn for double crochet, step two

Catch the yarn and draw it through the chain onto the hook (Fig. 4-22), which will leave three loops on the hook. Catch the yarn and draw it through the first two loops on the hook (Fig. 4-23). Catch the yarn again and draw it through the two remaining loops (Fig. 4-24) to complete one double crochet (Fig. 4-25). Repeat these steps in each of the remaining chains.

When you are ready to turn, add three chain stitches (Fig. 4-26) and reverse the fabric with the row just completed on top. Beginning with the double crochet, the turning chain becomes the first stitch of the second row. The three chains are equal to and count as one double crochet.

Wrap the hook and insert it under the top two threads of the second complete stitch of the preceding row (Fig. 4-27). Repeat the same steps as used in the first row for each row of double crochet.

You must be careful to complete the same number of stitches each time by putting the last stitch into the top of the chains which were counted as the first double crochet of the preceding row.

Ribbed double crochet

The ribbed double crochet is made with the same motions as the non-ribbed version but only one top thread is picked up as each stitch is begun.

Long double crochet. A row of double crochet has been included for contrast.

With regular double and triple crochet, after the initial loop is drawn onto the hook, each pair of loops drawn through makes the fabric in effect one row higher. The primary difference between double crochet and two rows of single crochet is the fact that there is no horizontal union between stitches, which creates vertical slits between them. This is the reason for loss of firmness in the fabric.

Long double crochet

There is a simple and interesting variation of the double crochet which is referred to as a long double crochet. It is made by starting from a foundation chain. Wrap the hook and insert it into the sixth chain from the hook (Fig. 4-28). Catch the yarn and draw a loop through onto the hook, expanding the loop and the wrap to a length of roughly three chains (Fig. 4-29). The stitch is then completed as though it were a regular double crochet, by catching the yarn and drawing it through two loops, two different times (Fig. 4-30).

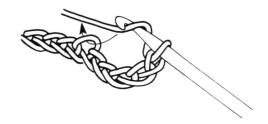

4-28 Insert for long double crochet

4-29. Long double crochet, step two

4-30. Long double crochet completed

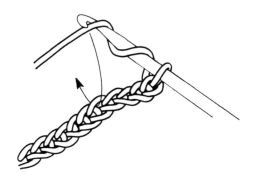

4-31. Insert for triple crochet

Triple crochet

Triple crochet is started from a foundation chain, with steps similar to those used for double crochet, and makes a stitch three rows high in one passage. Begin by wrapping the hook twice and inserting it from the front into the fifth chain from the hook (Fig. 4-31). Catch

Triple crochet

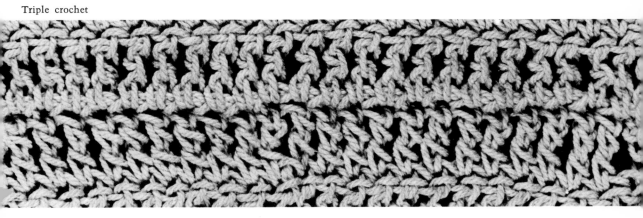

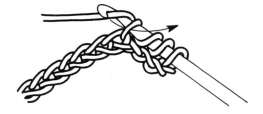

4-32. Triple crochet, step one

4-33. Triple crochet, step two

4-34. Triple crochet, step three

4-35. Triple crochet, step four

4-36. Triple crochet, completed

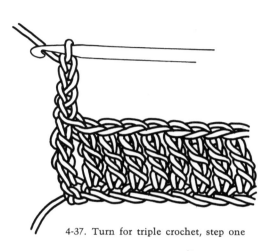

4-37. Turn for triple crochet, step one

the yarn and draw a loop through the chain and onto the hook (Fig. 4-32), leaving four loops on the hook. Catch the yarn and draw it through two loops, three different times (Figs. 4-33, 4-34, and 4-35), to complete one triple crochet (Fig. 4-36). Repeat these instructions for each of the remaining stitches on the foundation chain.

At the end of the row, add four chains (Fig. 4-37) and turn the fabric, keeping the stitches just completed on top. The four chains added are equal to and count as the first triple crochet of the second row. Wrap the hook twice and insert it under two threads of the second triple crochet of the preceding row (Fig. 4-38). Repeat the same steps as for the first row. Care should be taken to make the last triple crochet of each row in the top of the chains which act as the first triple crochet of the previous row.

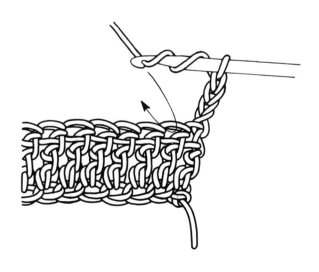

4-38. Turn for triple crochet, step two

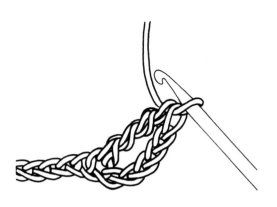

4-39. Double-triple crochet

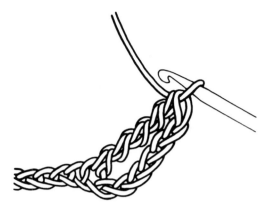

4-40. Triple-triple crochet

Ribbed triple crochet

As with the single and double crochet, the ribbed variation of the triple crochet is made by picking up only one top thread of each stitch of the previously completed rows.

Double-triple, triple-triple, and long triple crochet

There are still longer stitches referred to as double-triple, triple-triple, and long triple crochet. In each one of these stitches the same basic steps are used. However, with each successive stitch you add one more wrap around the hook before inserting it into the chain and you move the insertion one stitch farther down the chain. To turn, you also add one more stitch to the group of chains added to make the turn. For example, the double-triple crochet is made by wrapping the hook three times and inserting it into the sixth chain from the hook. Having drawn one loop onto the hook, draw through each pair of loops, four different times (Fig. 4-39). For the turn add five

chains, which are equal to and count as the first double-triple crochet of the second row. Insert into the second double-triple crochet of the preceding row to begin the second row. The triple-triple and long triple stitches follow the same pattern on up the scale. For example, you wrap four times for the triple-triple crochet. (Fig. 4-40).

Slip stitch

The slip stitch is another fundamental stitch. It has not been covered first in this section for the simple reason that it is a difficult stitch for beginners to handle. Once you've learned to manage the hook and yarn, the slip stitch is easy.

To make a slip stitch, insert the hook into the second stitch from the hook on the foundation chain. Catch the yarn and draw a loop through the chain stitch and the loop on the hook with one motion (Fig. 4-41). This completes one slip stitch (Fig. 4-42). Repeat this stitch for each of the remaining stitches on the foundation chain.

Slip stitch

4-41. Slip stitch, step one

4-42. Slip stitch, completed

4-44. Turn for slip stitch, step two

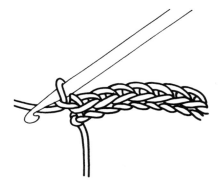

4-43. Turn for slip stitch, step one

When you are ready to turn, add one stitch (Fig. 4-43) and reverse the fabric so the row of stitches just completed is on top. Begin the next row by inserting the hook into one thread of the last complete stitch of the preceding row (Fig. 4-44). Continue with the same steps as used for the first row.

The slip stitch is the most dense of the fundamental crochet stitches. It only progresses a half-row of height at a time, with each row of stitches lying tightly on top of the last. Unless you are working with very large materials, the slip stitch is extremely slow. Nevertheless, this stitch is particularly desirable if you need an extremely firm body in the fabric you are making, especially for self-supporting soft sculptures. The slip stitch is also commonly used for joining loops or rows, as flexible reinforcement for edges, and for tapering or backtracking inconspicuously.

Half-double crochet

The half-double crochet is treated last because it is seldom used. It does, however, explain the technical gap between the single and double crochet. The half-double is a shortened version of the double crochet and consequently is one and one-half rows high.

The half-double crochet is started from a foundation chain. It is made by wrapping the hook and inserting it into the third chain from the hook (Fig. 4-45). Catch the yarn and draw a loop through the chain and onto the hook (Fig. 4-46), leaving three loops. Catch the yarn again and draw through all three loops in one

Half-double crochet

4-46. Half-double crochet, step two

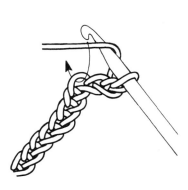

4-45. Insert for half-double crochet

4-47. Half-double crochet, completed

4-48. Turn for half-double crochet, step one

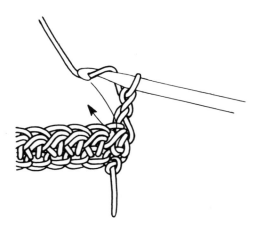

4-49. Turn for half-double crochet, step two

motion to complete a half-double crochet (Fig. 4-47). Repeat this stitch for each of the remaining chains.

To turn, add two chains (Fig. 4-48). These do not count as the first stitch of the second row, as they do with double and triple crochet. Wrap the hook and begin in the top of the last complete stitch of the preceding row (Fig. 4-49). Repeat the same steps for each succeeding row.

The following summary may help to clarify basic procedures.

stitch	wrap hook	begin in	to turn
slip stitch		2nd stitch from hook	chain 1
single crochet		2nd stitch from hook	chain 1
half double	once	3rd stitch from hook	chain 2
double crochet	once	4th stitch from hook	chain 3
triple crochet	twice	5th stitch from hook	chain 4
double triple	three times	6th stitch from hook	chain 5
triple triple	four times	7th stitch from hook	chain 6

5. TURNING, ENDING, AND CORRECTING

Turning

In regular crochet, there are basically two ways to build successive rows of stitches when you are working on a flat fabric. Turning or reversing the fabric is the simplest and most common approach. Ultimately both sides of the fabric have the same appearance because the rows are worked alternately from the front, from the back, from the front, and so on. This back and forth appearance becomes more evident with ribbed stitches, since the reversing creates alternating rows of ribs.

The second method is not actually a turn, but rather a return. In this method the face of the fabric does not change. It is done by cutting the yarn at the end of each row as though you were finishing, and beginning the next row in the first stitch of the row just completed. Since the fabric is not turned, it makes a distinct front and back. Here again, it is particularly distinguishable with the ribbed stitches since it leaves all ribs on one side of the fabric.

Ending

To finish off or end a piece, add a chain after you have finished the last stitch and draw it up into a long loop (Fig. 5-1). Cut the loop in the middle and draw the

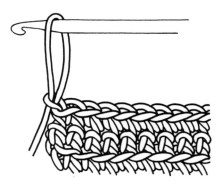

5-1. Drawing a long loop for ending

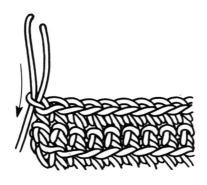

5-2. To complete ending, cut the loop and withdraw the source yarn

5-3. Drawing a long loop for temporary ending

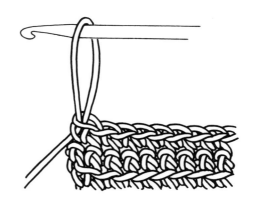

source yarn back out of the loop (Fig. 5-2). Pull the last stitch tight, and the end will not unravel. If you do not wish to use the tail end, and you choose to disguise it, it must be worked back into the fabric. This is best accomplished by weaving the end back through the last row, imitating the last few stitches until it becomes secure enough to cut. If you work with textured yarn or something "tacky," or nubbly, like wool or mohair, the end may become secure after working it through a few stitches. Slick materials may need to be extended farther into the fabric.

In some cases the beginning tail may be worked together with the source yarn as you make the foundation chain to actually finish off by making the tail part of the initial stitches, thus doubling up.

Temporary endings

To end a piece temporarily, do not add a chain but draw a long loop up at any point in the work (Fig. 5-3). Wrap it around the source yarn to tie a simple overhand knot (Fig. 5-4). This will keep it from unraveling until you can return to it. Later, simply untie the knot, slip the hook back into the loop, draw it back down onto the hook, and you are ready to continue.

Correcting

A mistake is only a mistake the first time. When you put it to work for you, the mistake becomes an invention. With crochet you are never dead-ended. You don't have to abandon a piece that you have put hours of work into—just take it apart and repair what you don't like!

One of the virtues of crochet is that it is all linked together, which allows you to back up and correct. Merely remove the hook from the work and unravel the crochet back to the point of correction by pulling on the yarn source. Then reinsert the hook and start anew.

If, after having begun a piece with a long foundation chain, you find that there are too many chains for the body of the work, the extra stitches can be removed. Simply untie the slip knot at the beginning of the chain and unravel stitches up to the body of the work.

Secure the tail end with a simple overhand knot. On the other hand, chains can be added to the foundation by joining in a new thread and crocheting as many stitches or pattern groups as you need.

Don't be discouraged if you have gone a long way with a piece and you want to make a correction at an earlier stage. You can remove a whole section of a piece and change it by actually cutting it out. Later you can join in another piece of crochet or a yarn to make a row of stitches to begin crocheting from. Cut the fabric and join the new yarn two rows above the cut edge to allow for some unraveling or shaggy edges. If the fabric unravels you can pull the yarn to a good clean edge and secure it by drawing the yarn through a loop as though you were ending. Then begin crocheting on the next row of stitches. If the fabric becomes shaggy on the edge, just turn under the shaggy part until you get a row of clean stitches, and add new yarn to this row with one of the joining techniques explained in Chapter 9.

5-4. To complete temporary ending, tie the loop around the source yarn in a simple overhand knot

6. CHANGING YARNS AND WORKING WITH COLOR

Changing yarns

There are three basic approaches to changing yarns: splicing, crocheting in, and tying in. Quite often during construction of a fabric you will either want to change color or you will run out of yarn on one skein and have to change to another. In both cases the following methods should be used.

Splicing

A simple splice is made by unraveling the plies at the ends of two threads and twisting them together into one yarn. If the yarn surface is nubbly or has tooth to it, just the twisting together of the plies will probably hold the splice. If the splice slips apart, perhaps a small amount of flexible fabric adhesive, available in sewing or notions departments of most stores, would prevent this from happening. For very large cords or rope, follow the directions in one of the many books available on splicing multi-strand cords.

Bulkiness in the splice may cause a lump that is undesirable, so the best approach is to plan ahead in order to avoid changing cords or splicing.

Crocheting in

Simply using two threads as one is the most basic method of crocheting in a new yarn. To do this, make one stitch with the starting and ending threads together. Then, drop the old thread and work with the new thread (Fig. 6-1). Later, the tail ends must be worked into the fabric until they become secure.

Another method of crocheting in that does not create an overlap, is to end off with one thread and begin with another. End one yarn as though you were finishing and begin a new one by drawing a slip knot onto the hook and inserting the hook into the next stitch as though you were working continuously. (Fig. 6-2). When working the next row, you must be careful to pick up both the ending stitch and the starting stitch to avoid

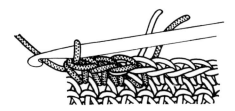

6-1. Changing yarns—using two threads as one

leaving a hole in the fabric. As with the previous technique, the tail ends must be worked back into the fabric until they are secure.

If you are making a flat fabric, as opposed to a sculptural form, this technique is best done at the side borders. It is easier to disguise with the ending yarn at one edge and the starting yarn at the other.

Still another way of changing yarns by crocheting is to lay the new yarn along the top of the previous row as you are crocheting. Work right around it as though it were part of the stitches. When you want to switch, pick up the new yarn to make one stitch. Cut the old yarn and lay it along the top edge of the previous row and crochet over it, using the new thread (Fig. 6-3). This actually works the ends in as you change yarns.

Tying in

To tie two cords together and continue crocheting as usual is referred to as tying

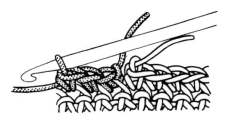

6-2. Changing yarns—ending one and starting another

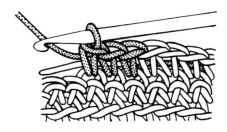

6-3. Changing yarns—crocheting over the new and old ends

in. Let the knot appear where it will for the moment and later untie it and work the ends into the crochet.

Working with color

The techniques used for changing colors are basically the same as those used for changing threads. By using the technique of combining two threads during the change, you can create a compound or blended color. This can be used to make a gradation between colors. To make this gradual change, work with two threads as one for several stitches or rows. (This is one of the methods referred to as crocheting in.)

If you do not want a gradation but prefer an abrupt change in the colors, crochet in by ending with one thread and starting with another or crocheting around the ends. These techniques, as well as tying in or splicing, will give you a clean color separation. You must, however, turn the colored tail ends of the joined threads back into the same-colored fabric as you work them in when finishing.

If a two-colored fabric is made with the color changing on a vertical line, an interlooping of colors is possible. Begin working with one color and switch to the second color while making the second half of a single crochet. Allowing the first yarn to hang free, continue with the new color. On the return row, make the switch back to the first color using the same procedure.

Stranding or floating

Stranding is a method of temporarily picking up alternating colors. It is usually employed on fabrics meant to be viewed from only one side, since there are threads that "float" across the back without being worked into the construction. Stranding is most appropriate for short color runs, usually a matter of a few stitches, and for switching back and forth between colors. It is best to wind the various colors on bobbins to prevent tangling.

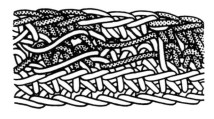

6-4. Stranding, back view

This temporary pick-up technique is done by crocheting with one color until you want to introduce another. Switch colors in the second half of a single crochet and merely drop the first color, allowing it to hang free until you need it again. Continue working with the second color until you want to return to the first. Switch back again by using the same steps as in the first change (Fig. 6-4).

With a one-sided fabric of this sort you can work with multiple strands using the temporary pick-up. This gives you an option of picking up any one thread or more than one thread at a time. With a very dense fabric or one in which a variegated surface is acceptable, it is possible to make a two-sided fabric using a variation of stranding in which the colors not being used become a cord over which the regular stitches are made.

Using two or more strands of different colors can create mottled or tweed effects. There may be times when there is no other way to get a particular color or effect than to combine two yarns. If you do, you must be careful not to cause problems by overloading the hook and splitting the yarns. Using a single variegated yarn is also another way to get a mottled color effect. There are many dyeing and overdyeing techniques which can be used with crochet. Consider the possibilities of dyeing yarns before or after making a piece, and of tie-dyeing and batiking completed pieces. You will soon realize that there are enough possibilities to fill another book.

7. OTHER STITCHES

An almost infinite variety of stitches can be created by combining the basic stitches in different ways. Only those fancy stitches that change the structure or surface of the fabric significantly will be covered here. If you are interested in learning more fancy stitches, there are several good books on how to do them listed in the Bibliography. However, you don't have to learn fancy stitches from books—you can also invent your own, since they are made from combinations of the basic stitches.

Beginning variables

Working "between stitches," "around the post or bar," and "into a space" refer to ways of inserting the hook other than

Filet crochet is made of open and filled squares. Pictures can be made and words can be spelled out in this way. Crocheted doily, circa 1915, 14 x 18 inches. Collection of Mr. and Mrs. O. E. Brown.

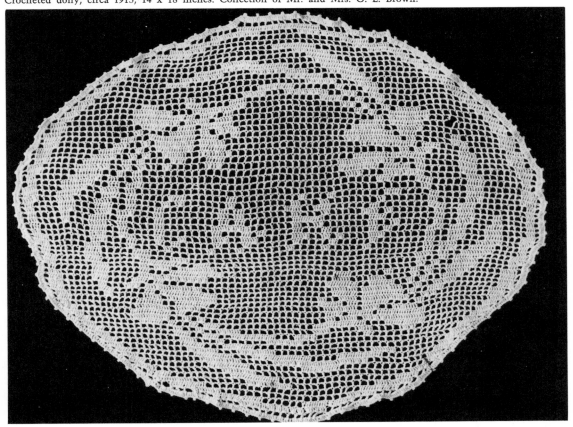

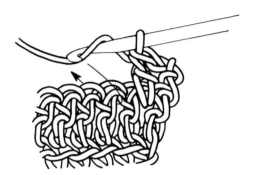

7-1. Working between stitches

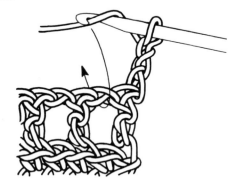

7-2. Working into a space

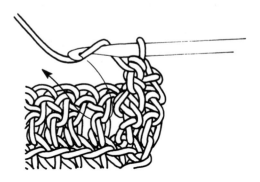

7-3. Working around the post

directly into the top of a stitch. To work between stitches means simply to insert from front to back into the small space between the stitches (Fig. 7-1). This differs from working in a space, since the "space" usually refers to one or more free chains inserted between regular stitches, thereby creating an opening, into which the hook is inserted (Fig. 7-2). To work around the post means to pass the hook behind the stitch. Insert it into the space at the right side of a stitch and back out at the left (Fig. 7-3). This method is used for creating relief in the surface texture.

The term "back to front" is occasionally used in making fancy stitches. It means to insert the hook directly in the top of the stitch, but from the back of the stitch to the front, or opposite from the usual direction.

Double chain

There are two types of foundation chains beside the single chain referred to earlier. You may want to consider them as alternative foundations or for use as trim. They are the double chain, sometimes referred to as a chain of single crochet, and the triple chain, occasionally known as a chain of double crochet.

The double chain is made by starting with a slip knot as for the single chain. Make two chain stitches. Insert the hook back into the first chain, catch the yarn and draw it through onto the hook (Fig. 7-4). Catch the yarn again and draw it

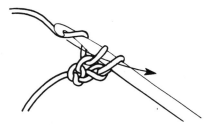

7-4. Double-chain stitch, step one

Double chain

7-5. First double-chain stitch completed

through both loops on the hook as though you are making a single crochet (Fig. 7-5).

Next, insert the hook under the left loop of the two loops just slipped off the hook (Fig. 7-6). Catch the yarn and draw it through and onto the hook, which leaves two loops (Fig. 7-7). (This motion

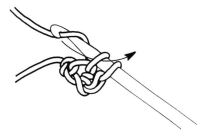

7-6. Insert for second double-chain stitch

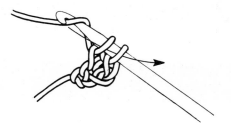

7-7. Second double-chain stitch, step one

7-8. Second double-chain stitch, completed

may look as if you are drawing the yarn back out of the stitch.) Catch the yarn again and draw through both loops to complete the second double chain stitch (Fig. 7-8). Repeat the steps from the pick-up of the left loop to make the chain the desired length.

The use of the double chain by itself makes a good linear element or a substantial cord that can be used as finishing trim. If you use a double chain for the foundation of a fabric and you work the first row of stitches on the edge with the large loops, it looks somewhat like a corded edge. To use a double chain as a foundation, add one or more single chains to bring the yarn to the proper height for the stitch you have chosen, as you do for turning.

Triple chain

A triple chain is made by beginning with three chain stitches and wrapping the yarn around the hook once before inserting it into the first chain. Catch the yarn and draw it through onto the hook, leaving three loops. Catch the yarn again and draw it through each pair of

Triple chain

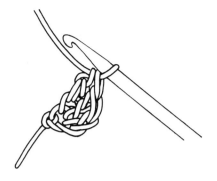

7-10. Triple chain stitch, completed

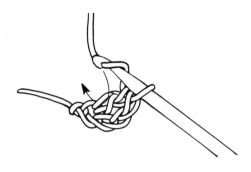

7-9. Insert for triple chain stitch

loops, in effect making a double crochet.

Next, wrap the yarn once around the hook and insert it into the very left or bottom loop created by the first double crochet (Fig. 7-9). Catch the yarn and draw it through onto the hook. Catch the yarn again and draw it through each two loops to complete the second triple chain (Fig. 7-10). Repeat the directions from the point of inserting the hook into the far left loop of the last complete stitch. As in the double chain, this makes a wide band or strip of crochet that can be used as an element by itself or as a wide foundation chain.

Joined double crochet

In the description of the basic stitches, the double and triple crochets were described as having no horizontal or lateral

Joined double crochet

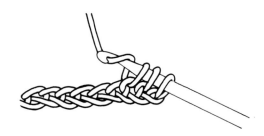

7-11. Joined double crochet, step one

7-12. First joined double crochet, completed

union, causing the fabric to be more pliable or flexible than the same yarn crocheted in single crochets. There is a stitch that joins double and triple crochets, replacing some of the firmness or body normally lost with these stitches. This stitch is called the joined double or joined triple crochet.

A joined double crochet is made by starting from a foundation chain and inserting the hook into the second chain from the hook. Catch the yarn and draw it through onto the hook. Insert the hook into the next stitch, catch the yarn, and bring it through onto the hook, making three loops (Fig. 7-11). Next, catch the yarn and draw it through two of the loops. Catch it again and draw it through the two remaining loops. This completes the first joined double crochet (Fig. 7-12).

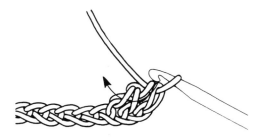

7-13. First insert for second joined double crochet

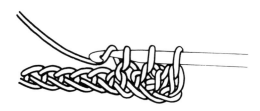

7-14. Second insert for second joined double crochet

7-15. Second joined double crochet completed

Begin the second joined stitch by inserting the hook under the left loop of the first stitch (Fig. 7-13). Catch the yarn and draw it through onto the hook. Insert the hook into the next chain stitch, catching the yarn and drawing it also onto the hook, leaving three loops (Fig. 7-14). As in the last stitch, this stitch is completed by drawing a loop through each pair of loops on the hook (Fig. 7-15).

Repeat the directions, picking up the left loop and one chain for each stitch to complete the row. To turn, add two chains and pick up the first chain and the top of the last complete double crochet.

Joined triple crochet

The procedure for making a joined triple crochet is similar to that of the joined double crochet. Insert the hook into the

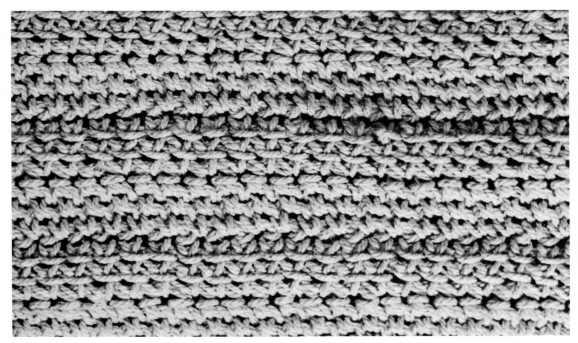

Joined triple crochet

7-16. Joined triple crochet, step one

7-17. First joined triple crochet, completed

first, second, and third chains, catching the yarn each time, and drawing it onto the hook (Fig. 7-16). Then, with four loops on the hook, catch the yarn and draw it through each pair, three different times, to complete the first joined triple crochet (Fig. 7-17).

To make the second stitch, insert the hook into the top left loop of the first complete stitch and draw a loop through onto the hook. Next, insert the hook into the bottom loop of the same stitch and draw another loop onto the hook (Fig. 7-18). Then, insert into the next chain stitch, catching the yarn and drawing another loop onto the hook, leaving four loops. Complete the stitch by drawing a loop through each pair of loops. (Fig. 7-19). Repeat these steps, picking up two loops and one chain for each stitch until the row is completed.

Begin the first stitch of the second row by adding three chains to turn, and pick up the second and first chains, and the top of the last complete stitch of the previous row. Continue, using the same steps as for the first row.

Filet crochet

Since double and triple crochets are in effect bars of stitches with no lateral union, they have vertical slits between them. If the vertical slits are enlarged by spacing the stitches, they will create a gridwork known as simple filet crochet or square mesh. Traditional filet is made

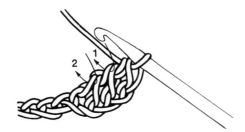

7-18. Second insert for second joined triple crochet

7-19. Second joined triple crochet, completed

7-20. Traditional filet crochet

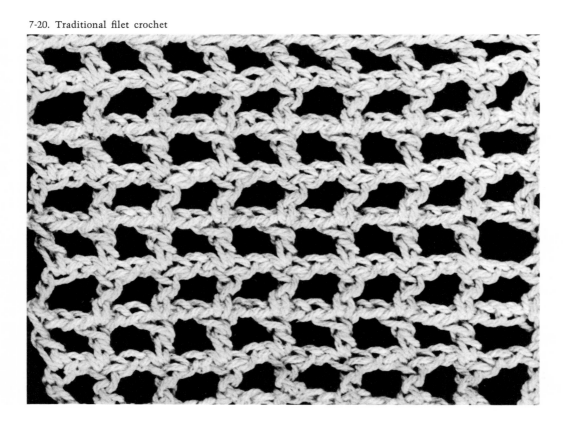

by using double crochet and making square openings (Fig. 7-20).

The spacing is achieved by adding one or more chains between stitches and skipping a corresponding number on the foundation chain or previous row. These openings can be made into long, narrow slots or square, rectangular, or triangular spaces. Any stitch longer than a single crochet can be used. For example, when working with double crochet, if you add two chains before starting a stitch and skip two stitches of the preceding row,

you will end up with a square opening. The opening is two stitches high (double crochet) and two stitches wide (two chains at the top and bottom) and the same number of stitches as in the previous row is maintained. This grid or mesh is the most basic characteristic of filet crochet.

You will often find a pictorial approach to filet crochet which utilizes bars of double crochet within this mesh to make images from solid areas contrasted with open spaces (Fig. 7-21). There are many

7-21. Pictorial approach to filet crochet. Bars of double crochet within the mesh contrast with open spaces (Courtesy of O. E. Brown)

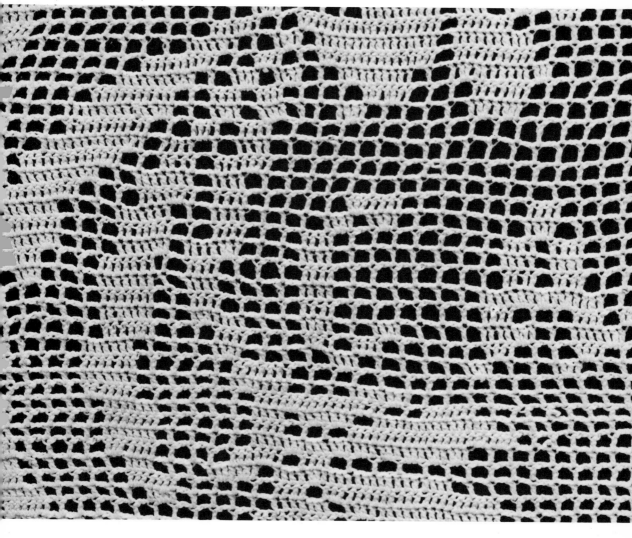

Arc stitch

good sources of information on how to do filet crochet, including some of those in the Bibliography.

Openings of unusual shapes can be made by varying the number of stitches picked up or skipped. A horizontal rectangle can be made by using double crochet and skipping three or more spaces between. Using triple crochet presents still more possibilities. Alternating triangles can be made by adding no chains at the top and skipping two or three stitches at the bottom and then reversing that by adding two or three chains at the top and skipping no stitches at the bottom. With experimentation you will find many other possibilities.

Arc or arch stitch

An arc stitch is another simple and effective way to make an open meshwork. Make a foundation chain and begin by putting a single crochet in the second stitch from the hook. Make a chain of five stitches and, skipping two stitches on the foundation chain, make a single crochet into the third. Next, chain five stitches and skip three on the foundation. Single crochet into the fourth. Repeat these steps, skipping three chains until the first row is completed.

To turn, chain five stitches and then join the chains to the center of each arc by making one single crochet into the center stitch of the five-chain arc from the previous row. Continue making five chains and single crocheting into the center stitch of each arc.

Beginning with a turning chain of five, finish the last row by making three chains and joining them, as above, to the center of each arc. This step is a repetition of what was done in the other rows, but you only make three chains between each single crochet.

Check stitch

The check stitch is still another style of open meshwork, with a little more body to it, that has become popular in easy-

Check stitch

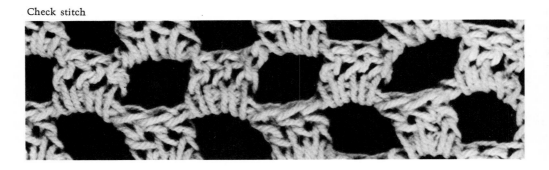

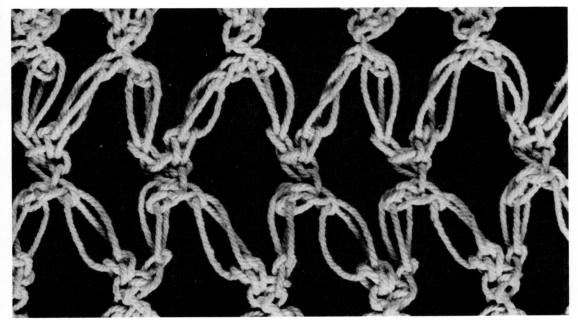

Knot stitch

to-make fashions. The check stitch is made on a foundation chain. Begin with a double crochet in the fourth chain from the hook and another double crochet in the fifth. Next, chain three, and skipping three on the foundation chain, put a double crochet into the fourth chain. Make a double crochet into each of the next two chains. Continue this pattern of making three double crochets and a three-chain space across the entire length of the row, ending with a group of three double crochets.

To begin the second row, make six chains and turn. In the first space of the previous row, make three double crochets, working around the chain. Continue, making three double crochets in each three-chain space of the previous row, and three chain spaces between. To form the last space in the second row which comes above the check, make two chains and a double crochet into the top of the last stitch of the previous row.

To begin row three, chain three, turn, and make two double crochets in the space just made in the previous row. Repeat these steps for each succeeding row.

Knot stitch

To make a knot stitch, start with a foundation chain in multiples of five stitches. Begin the first row of knot stitches by pulling up a long loop, about the length of three or four chains on the foundation (Fig. 7-22). Catch the yarn and draw it through the long loop, which makes a small loop or wrap around the hook.

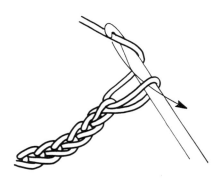

7-22. Drawing a long loop for knot stitch

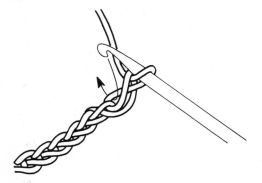

7-23. Knot stitch, step one

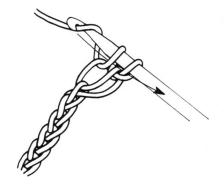

7-24. Knot stitch, step three

7-25. Knot stitch, completed

7-26. Double-knot stitch, completed by a single crochet and joined to foundation

Insert the hook between the long loop and the single strand (Fig. 7-23). Catch the yarn and draw it onto the hook, which leaves two loops (Fig. 7-24). Catch the yarn again and draw it through both loops, which secures the first single knot stitch (Fig. 7-25). This sequence, in effect, makes a single crochet.

A double-knot stitch is made by drawing up another loop of approximately the same length, and repeating the same steps used to secure the first knot stitch. Then join the double-knot stitch to the foundation chain by skipping four chain stitches and inserting the hook into the fifth chain, and making a single crochet

7-27. Turn for double-knot stitch, step two

(Fig. 7-26). Continue making double-knot stitches and joining them to every fifth chain on the foundation until you have completed the first row.

To turn, make a triple-knot stitch and reverse the work with the row just completed on top. Join the triple stitch to the single crochet at the center of the last double knot stitch of the previous row, using a single crochet (Fig. 7-27). Continue making double-knot stitches and joining them to the center of each knot stitch, in succession, of the previous row. Repeat these steps for each of the following rows.

There is a knot-stitch technique that will give a heavier knot at the center. If you want to do this, the heavier knot is made after turning the work to make the second row. Rather than make one single crochet at the center of the knot stitch, make two, one on either side of the knot (the single crochet at the center). The hook is inserted between the long loop and the single strand to do this.

Simple cluster stitch

The concept of compounding stitches into clusters is one which has many variations. The simple cluster stitch begins with a

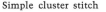
Simple cluster stitch

7-28. Simple cluster stitch, step one

7-29. Cluster stitch, completed

foundation chain. The first cluster is started by making three double crochets in the fourth stitch from the hook, each time leaving the last loop on the hook. To do this, wrap the hook and insert it into the stitch, drawing a loop onto the hook. Catch the yarn and draw through two loops, leaving the last two loops on the hook. Repeat this two more times, leaving the last loop on the hook each time, which will leave four loops on the hook (Fig. 7-28). Complete the cluster by drawing a loop through all four loops at once and lock it with a chain stitch (Fig. 7-29).

Adding two chains and skipping two chains on the foundation, make a cluster of three double crochets in the next stitch. Continue making spaced clusters across

the whole first row. When the last cluster is completed, chain three and turn.

Make the second row by putting clusters of three double crochets into the spaces created by the chains between clusters in the first row. At the end of the second row and all succeeding rows, make the last cluster in the space between the turning chain and the first cluster, so you end up with the same number of clusters in the second row as you had in the first.

There are a great number of variations of the cluster stitch, and this is only a simple one. The number of stitches in a cluster can vary, the height of stitch can vary (i.e., double, triple, etc.), and spacing between clusters can vary. As well as being used separately as a fancy stitch,

Pineapple, or puff, stitch

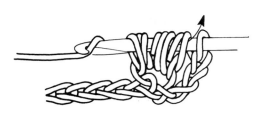

7-30. Pineapple stitch, step one

7-31. Pineapple stitch, completed

the cluster stitch can also be used as an overlay, working over a fabric groundwork of other stitches.

Pineapple stitch or puff stitch

An unusual variation of the cluster stitch is the pineapple stitch. It is also made from a foundation chain. Begin by wrapping the hook and inserting it into the fifth chain from the hook, to draw up a long loop (approximately the length of three or four chain stitches). Wrap the hook, insert it in the same stitch, and draw up another long loop. Repeat this procedure a total of four times, so that you end up with nine loops on the hook (Fig. 7-30). Catch the yarn and draw it through eight loops, leaving two on the hook. Catch the yarn again and draw it

through the two remaining loops, which will lock the stitch (Fig. 7-31). Chain one and skip one chain on the foundation. Continue to make clusters in every other stitch with a space between.

To begin the second row, turn by adding four chains. Make the clusters of long loops in the chain spaces of the previous row. Include the space at the end of the row, made by the turning chain from the first row, so you finish with the same number of clusters in each row.

Popcorn stitch

The popcorn stitch is an overlay stitch that creates great knobs on the surface of the fabric. It is done basically by making a cluster over a fabric of single and dou-

Popcorn stitch

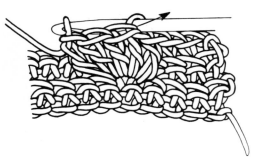

7-32. Popcorn stitch, step one

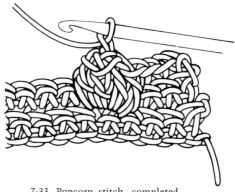

7-33. Popcorn stitch, completed

ble crochets. Begin by making a chain and three rows of ribbed single crochet, working in the back loop only (the top stitch farthest away from you). Start the fourth row by making three single crochets, again working in the back loop. Begin the popcorn cluster by making five double crochets in the front loop of the fifth single crochet of the *first* row, actually working over the top of the fabric. When you have completed the fifth double crochet, remove the hook and insert it into the top of the first double crochet and the top of the fifth, which is the loop you dropped. (Fig. 7-32). Draw the loop of the fifth double crochet through the first and then make one chain to close the cluster (Fig. 7-33). Skip one stitch of the previous row and, again working in the back loop, make one single crochet in the next five stitches. Then begin the next popcorn cluster in the first row, having skipped five stitches to correspond with the five single crochets just made. Repeat this sequence until the first row is completed.

The next row is made of single crochets worked in the back loop. Make certain that you pick up only the one closing

stitch of the popcorn as you work back across, to maintain an even number of stitches. The succeeding row is made by working into the third row on the front of the fabric and spacing the popcorns alternately so they will fall between the popcorns previously made. Alternate each popcorn row with one row of single crochet made in the back loop.

Loop stitch

You can make pile or shag in crochet with a loop stitch. The traditional loop stitch is an unsecured type of stitch that can be pulled apart or separated. Since many of the works you may want to make will have tension or weight on them, the following instructions are for a secured loop stitch.

To make a loop stitch, begin with a foundation chain and one row of single crochets. Chain one and turn. Wrap the yarn around your index finger or a piece of cardboard, in the opposite direction from the way you normally would, passing the yarn behind the finger and then forward. Insert the hook into the first stitch, and pass it to the right and over the strand that goes behind your finger

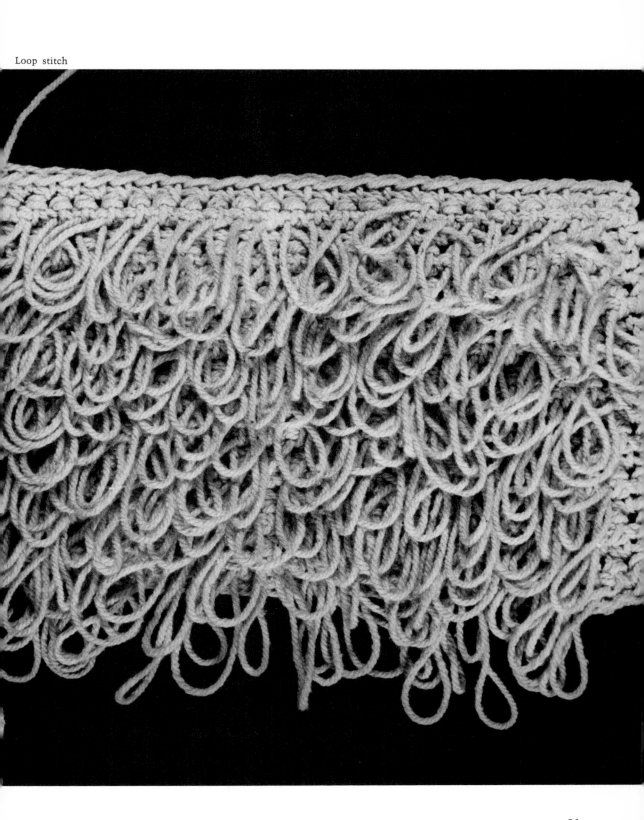

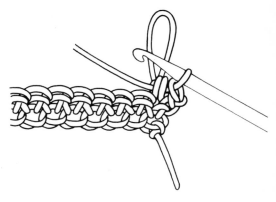

7-36. Loop stitch, completed

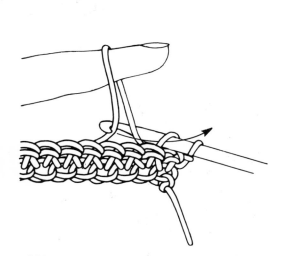

7-34. Loop stitch, step one

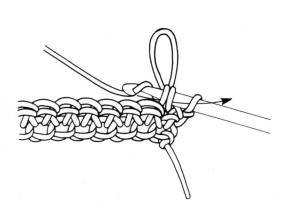

7-35. Loop stitch, step two

(Fig. 7-34). Catch the yarn that comes over your finger, and pull both yarns through the stitch and onto the hook (Fig. 7-35). Drop the loop and complete the stitch with one motion, catching the yarn as you normally would and drawing it through all three loops on the hook (Fig. 7-36). Repeat the same steps for each of the remaining single crochets.

Chain one to turn, and alternate each row of loop stitches with a row of single crochets. The loops can be left as loops or cut for appearance.

The loop stitch makes a flat fabric with loops, or pile, in alternating rows. The loop stitch itself forms a loop on the back of the fabric and a single crochet on the front. The single crochet appears different because the first motion brings two loops onto the hook rather than the normal one.

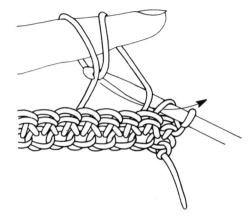

7-37. Double-loop stitch, step one

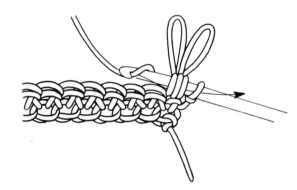

7-38. Double-loop stitch, step two

Double-loop stitch

A double-loop stitch is made with the same steps as the single-loop stitch, except that the yarn is wrapped around your index finger twice, to make two loops.

Begin with a foundation chain and one row of single crochets. Insert the hook into the first stitch and pass it to the right and over the yarn. Pass the hook from right to left through the loop on your finger (Fig. 7-37). Catch both cords and bring all three strands through the stitch (Fig. 7-38). Complete the stitch by catching the yarn as you normally would and bring it through all the loops on the hook. This makes a secured double-loop stitch (Fig. 7-39).

As with the single-loop stitch, you must alternate rows of loop stitches with rows of single crochets. You can make the

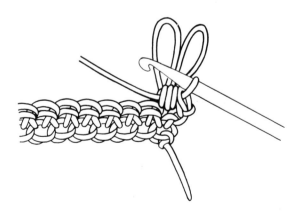

7-39. Double-loop stitch, completed

Bullion bar

loops as long as you wish by drawing down on the loop when the hook is passed through it. Let the yarn slide over your finger until the loops reach the desired length. Complete the stitch as described.

Bullion bar

There is a unique stitch, known in Europe as the bullion bar, that is made essentially from a long single crochet drawn through a series of wraps around the hook.

To do the bullion stitch you *must* have a tapered hook which is thinner toward the hook end of the tool, such as the "bone" type of plastic hook that is available today.

Begin by making a chain. Wrap the yarn around the hook eight times and insert it into the fifth chain from the hook. Catch the yarn and draw a loop onto the hook (Fig. 7-40). Catch the yarn again and draw it through all but the last loop of the wrapping. Complete the stitch by drawing a loop through both of the remaining loops. (Fig. 7-41). Follow these same steps in each chain on the foundation.

7-40. Bullion bar, step one

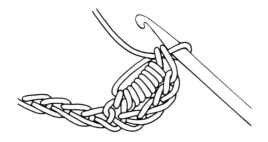

7-41. Bullion bar, completed

8. SHAPING

With most crocheted pieces you can make a form or shape by working continuously and do the shaping by increasing and decreasing. The shape a fabric takes is determined by where the changes are placed. Where shapes are made by joining two pieces, the union can be made so that it is not visible and the piece appears to be continuous. Joining methods are discussed in Chapter 9.

Increasing and decreasing

There are three possible ways of increasing and decreasing with all regular crochet stitches. One method, the second described here, is most commonly used, es-

Detail of a tubular crochet sculpture with three-dimensional ruffles. Sample by Linda Valeri

8-1. Increasing by adding stitches

8-2. Decreasing by skipping stitches

8-3. Increasing by making a double stitch

pecially with stitches higher than single crochet, but the others offer suitable alternatives. Each method of increasing has a complementary method of decreasing. Each pair will be described together.

Adding between stitches or skipping stitches

The simplest technique used to increase is one in which a chain stitch is placed between stitches (Fig. 8-1). This creates two stitches where there was originally only one. The extra chain will be picked up in the following row as though it were a separate stitch. For each chain added you will have increased by one stitch.

To skip a stitch each time you want to decrease, the counterpart of the increasing method, reduces the number of stitches by one for each stitch skipped (Fig. 8-2).

You may choose not to use this method of increasing and decreasing because it forms a small hole in the fabric that becomes more obvious as you increase the height of the stitch to double or triple crochet. If you are making a porous fabric, a small hole may not be a problem, but if you are making a fine, closely crocheted fabric, the space may spoil the appearance.

Working in one stitch or combining stitches

This traditional method of increasing and decreasing is most commonly used because it leaves little evidence of change. To increase, merely make a double stitch, putting two stitches in one chain or stitch of the previous row (Fig. 8-3). With each double stitch you are increasing by one stitch.

The counterpart of the double stitch is

to decrease by combining two stitches into one. Make two half-stitches and draw them together, thereby reducing one stitch for each two combined.

With single crochet this is done by inserting the hook into a stitch and drawing a loop onto the hook. Without completing the stitch, insert the hook into the next stitch and draw another loop onto the hook, making two half single crochets. Complete the decrease by catching the yarn again and drawing it through all three loops on the hook, which combines the two stitches into one (Fig. 8-4).

For decreasing double and triple crochet, the same basic process is used. Bring two stitches to the point where the last loop of each remains on the hook along with the original loop. Then draw both stitches together into one (Figs. 8-5 and 8-6).

Working at the edge of the fabric

The third method of increasing and decreasing is done at the edges of the fabric or ends of a row. This method

8-4. Decreasing by making two half stitches (single crochet)

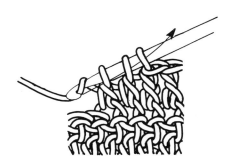

8-5. Decreasing by making two half stitches (double crochet)

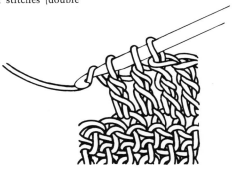

8-6. Decreasing by making two half stitches (triple crochet)

8-7. Increasing by adding at the row's edge

8-8. Decreasing by not working out to the edge

makes a characteristic step-out at the edge.

An increase is made by adding extra chains at either end of the row and beginning the stitches in the extra chains (Fig. 8-7). The row will be increased by one stitch for each chain added beyond the number required to turn. This will create a step increase.

A decrease with the same visual effect can be made by not working to the end of each row of stitches. By turning at a point short of the last stitch in a row or making slip stitches at the beginning, you will create the same step decrease (Fig. 8-8). The row will be decreased by one stitch for each stitch not completed.

The placement of increases and decreases and the rate at which they are made will have a significant effect on the object you are making. Evenly spaced increases or decreases make smooth transitions. An evenly spaced change is made by increasing or decreasing in every stitch or by spacing them at regular intervals such as every second, third, or fourth stitch. If the changes are unevenly spaced, they make lumpy, rough surfaces. An uneven change refers to a random increase or decrease.

The rate of change is determined by the spacing, or lack of it, between each increase or decrease. The rate of increase is doubled if you put two stitches in each stitch of the previous row, halved if you put two stitches in every other stitch, and so on. The rate ranges from gradual—putting one or more regular stitches between each increase or decrease—to rapid—making one or more increases or decreases in every stitch.

The rate at which increases and decreases are made will change the structure of the fabric, creating curves or arcs, ruffles, and gathers. In three dimensions the same changes make domes, bulges, and corners.

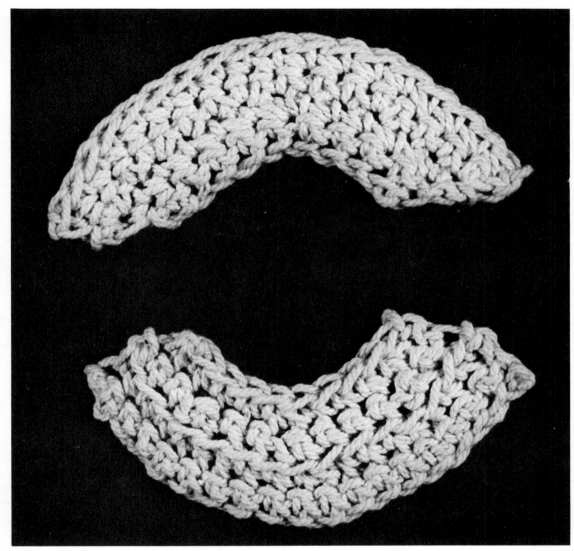

Curve or arc

Curve or arc

A curve or an arc is made in a flat piece by starting from a foundation chain and gradually increasing the number of stitches in each successive row. Increasing makes an arc with the wide part at the top of the fabric. Conversely, decreasing very gradually makes an arc with the wide part at the bottom, farthest away from the row you are working on.

Ruffle and gather

The same general technique described above applies to making a ruffle or gather, but the rate of change is much more intensive, faster than the fabric can handle and still remain flat. A ruffle is made at the edge of a fabric by increasing very rapidly, which overloads the previously made stitches until they buckle. A gather is made by decreasing enough to shorten the edge of the fabric, consequently gathering or puckering the fabric behind it.

Wall hanging by Carole Beadle uses arc and ruffles

9. JOINING

Joining can be done in many ways in crochet. Two crocheted fabrics can be joined by crocheting or sewing them together. They can be joined at the edges or an edge of one can be joined to the surface of another. Non-crocheted as well as crocheted fabrics can be joined with crochet stitches, and yarn can be joined to a fabric to make a ridge or a new surface. If separate pieces that need blocking or shaping are being joined, it is best to block them before joining them.

To join two fabrics with crochet stitches, place them face-to-face, with the backs outward. Draw a slip knot onto the hook and insert the hook into one stitch taken from the edge of each fabric. Treating the two stitches as one, join them with a slip stitch, drawing through both stitches and the loop on the hook at once (Fig. 9-1). Continue working along the edges, picking up one stitch from each fabric until you have completed the union. Since the fabrics have been crocheted together, the two become one, both structurally and visually.

If the stitches are not the same size, you may need to join two or more small stitches to each large stitch. To prevent buckling at one edge, pick up each small stitch separately, judging how many to join to each large stitch by estimating the relative lengths of the two pieces.

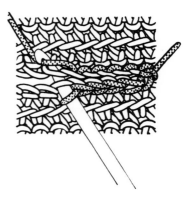

9-1. Joining one edge to another with a slip stitch

Wall Hanging No. 7, Isolde Savage, 88 inches, jute twine. A design in relief is created by joining and ridges. (Photo by Savage)

Joining can be done to provide a new surface (such as
the center ruffled addition) or as reinforcement on the
edge of a ruffle or ring of yarn (as at the bottom).
(Photo by Robert Burningham)

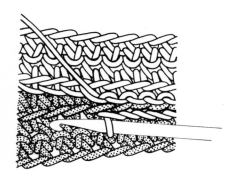

9-2. Joining an edge to a flat surface with a slip stitch

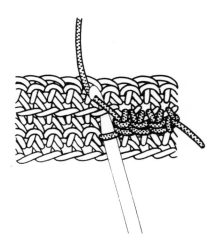

9-3. Building the foundation for a new surface on a flat surface

If you choose to make a ridge along the joint, turn the fabrics face out and follow the same steps as above, using a single or double crochet to join the pieces. This will make a raised seam where the two fabrics join.

Joining can be done of course by sewing as well as crocheting. To do this, place the front sides of the fabric together and pin them so the surfaces are flat. Sew the edges together with a whip stitch or back stitch, using the same yarn used in the fabric and a yarn needle. Try to make the sewing as inconspicuous as possible, perhaps using no knots and sewing right through the ply of the yarn. You must be careful not to stitch too tightly, which will gather the edge, or too loosely, which will permit the seam to pull apart, especially if you are working with elastic materials.

Joining the edge of a fabric to the flat surface of another can be done by picking up one stitch from the edge of the piece you are adding and one stitch from the surface of the second fabric at a point where you want to join them. Draw the loops together with a slip stitch (Fig. 9-2). Continue picking up one stitch from each until the two are joined, edge to surface.

A ridge, a new surface, or a dimensional form can be built off the surface of a fabric. Merely draw a slip knot onto the hook and arbitrarily pick up any stitch of the fabric as though it were a foundation chain. You are free to select whatever stitch you wish to start building with. By continuing to pick up a succession of stitches in this way, you create an edge that will stand away from the original fabric. (Fig. 9-3). This row can serve as the foundation for building any form possible to make with crochet.

Crocheting onto a non-crocheted surface such as a woven, knitted, or macramé fabric is also possible if the stitches are large enough to get the hook under. Follow any of the methods previously suggested and pick up each stitch as though it were crocheted.

With each of the techniques covered so far you must insert the hook into the stitches in order to begin working. If the stitches or the weave of the fabric are too fine, sew a row of stitches—any stitch or loop you can get the hook under will work—onto the fabric using the crochet yarn and making the stitches large enough to allow the hook to pass under them easily. Use this row as a foundation from which to begin crocheting. This method forms a strong union between the new crocheted surface and the fine fabric.

10. FINISHING

Finishing can make or break a piece, so don't slight this final phase of your work. Since crochet is essentially a four-selvedged technique, it presents few of the finishing problems of other textile techniques. You do, however, have the option of adding finishing effects. Fringe, armatures, and reinforcements are largely a matter of personal taste, and can be broadly varied in their interpretations.

Crocheted edges

There are several ways of giving a fabric a crocheted finish that will make the edges or rims more rigid than the fabric edge alone. This can be simply done by using slip stitches in the last row or two when making a piece, or by adding them to a finished fabric. Slip stitches make a clean, crisp edge. A double slip-stitched edge can be made by crocheting over the top of the first slip-stitched edge with another row or round of slip stitches. If the second round is made from left to right, opposite in direction from the usual row, it creates an even heavier corded effect. (Fig. 10-1).

An effect similar to the double slip-stitched edge can be created by crocheting around the fabric, in whatever stitch was used, with a double or triple yarn.

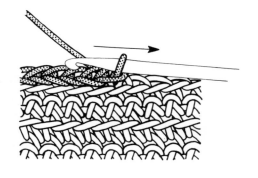

10-1. Slip-stitched edge made by crocheting in reverse direction

This medusa-like piece by Jane Knight, wool, 12 x 48 inches, employs curled free foundation chains. After the desired length has been reached, the artist crocheted back up the chain with single crochet stitches. (Photo by Jane Knight)

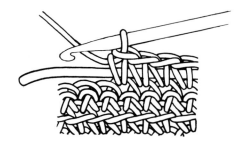

10-2. Corded edge made by crocheting around a cord

You can make a corded edge by laying a cord or several strands of yarn along the top edge of the fabric to be finished and crocheting through the edge stitches and around the cord as though the cord were part of the stitches (Fig. 10-2).

An undulating edge can be made by using a progression of changes in the height of stitches, from short ones to long ones and back to short.

Fringes

Fringes of plain yarn can easily be looped into crocheted fabric edges. Cut one or more pieces of yarn for the fringe that are double the length of the intended fringe, and fold them in half. Insert the hook through an edge stitch, draw the fringe yarns through the fabric by the fold (just far enough to make a loop sufficient to bring the ends of the yarn through), and pull tight (Fig. 10-3).

Crocheted fringes, which tend to curl slightly, can also be made by starting a chain from one of the edge stitches. Make a chain off from the stitch as you would make a foundation chain. Continue making separate chains until you

A

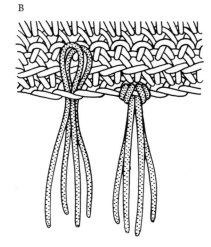

B

10-3. Fringing shown from the front (A) and the back (B)

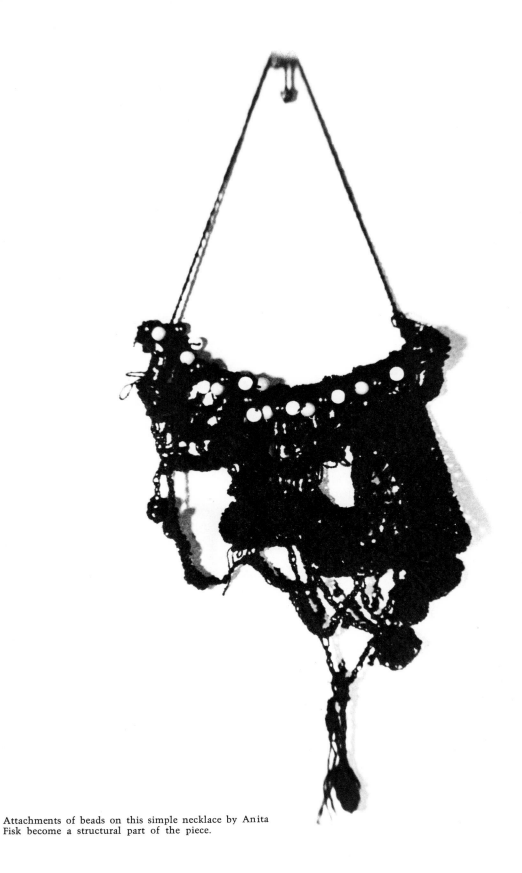

Attachments of beads on this simple necklace by Anita
Fisk become a structural part of the piece.

have the number of fringes you want. The spiraling or curling will depend on the nature of the materials used and the tension applied while making the chains.

If you desire a heavier fringe, make a foundation chain and then a row of slip stitches back toward the fabric. A still heavier fringe, which will spiral even more, is made by crocheting a foundation chain and then a row of single crochets back toward the fabric using a fair amount of tension. When making the single crochets, the fringe can be made very curly by increasing as you head back.

Attachments

Beads, bones, and other objects can be attached to crochet by stringing the articles on the source yarn before you begin to crochet. Allow the articles to slide onto the source yarn away from the work. To make threading easier, dip the end of the yarn in wax to stiffen it. Since the attachment will naturally come out on the back side of the fabric as you work, you should work from the back side so that the attachment falls on the front. As you need the object, merely slide it forward, next to the work. Catch the yarn just

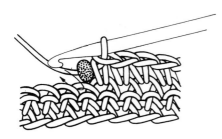

10-4. Crocheting in attachments

beyond the attachment to make the next stitch (Fig. 10-4), which locks the object in position.

Other surface additions such as embroidery or stitchery present still further possibilities.

Blocking

Blocking is a finishing technique used to shape fabrics after they have been crocheted and possibly pulled out of shape during construction. The process includes several basic steps, but the way you approach them will depend on the scale of your work. Obviously you cannot handle a large rope wall hanging with the same apparatus used for a typical garment. There may be some items, particularly garments or flat square or rectangular items, that you can get blocked professionally.

For unusual shapes you'll have to do the blocking yourself. In many cases there will be suggestions for blocking and washing the materials on the wrapper when you buy your yarn. Don't run the risk of ruining your work in this final stage. Check if you are unsure.

Basic steps for blocking include (1) laying out the final dimensions or shape of the piece, (2) wetting the fabric, (3) laying or pinning it onto a form, and (4) allowing it to dry. In some cases it may suffice to steam the fabric, using a hand steamer or a steam iron held lightly over the work. A dampened cloth placed over the piece and then ironed lightly with a regular iron may also work. Whether steaming or wetting, you allow the piece to dry completely. Do not try to hurry the drying by placing the piece in direct sunlight or very near a heat source such as a radiator. This will often shrink or unnecessarily fade the fabric.

For lightweight or small fabrics which do not need to be stretched, a flat surface covered with toweling is all you need. After wetting the fabric and squeezing the excess moisture out, you can merely lay out the fabric with the back side up, to the proper shape and size, and then allow to dry.

For fabrics that need to be stretched use a backboard soft enough to take pins or tacks, such as composition board or plastic foam insulation board. On a piece of heavy paper, outline the final shape of your piece and tack this onto the board. At this point you may want to cover the board and sketch with a clear sheet of plastic which will save your materials from being water-soaked. Next, wet the fabric and squeeze the excess moisture out. Then, using rust-proof pins or tacks, fasten it to the backboard in the shape of the sketch. Pin it at about 1"-1½" intervals around the perimeter and at any other point vital to forming the final shape. Be careful not to scallop the edges.

With some ingenuity and effort the same approach can be applied to three-dimensional forms. Very large pieces, however, often pose problems in carpentry. To block properly, you may need a wooden backboard or form to which the fabric can be nailed. Large pieces can be wet with a spray bottle, a squeeze bottle, or perhaps even a hose, and then allowed to dry.

11. GEOMETRIC SHAPES AND THREE-DIMENSIONAL FORMS

Crochet, as a single-element fabric-construction techniques, is one of the simplest techniques to use for making shapes and three-dimensional forms in varied ways. You may want to begin by making some of the geometric forms and assembling them into closed shapes, or you may want to build as you go by doing free-form or random crochet.

Although this chapter contains basic directions for making geometric shapes, the principles involved are far more important than the specifics. Since there is no recommendation made for specific materials and tools, you will have to vary the number of stitches, rows, etc. in your particular piece to accommodate your particular needs.

Disc made by the spiraling method   Disc made by intersecting each round

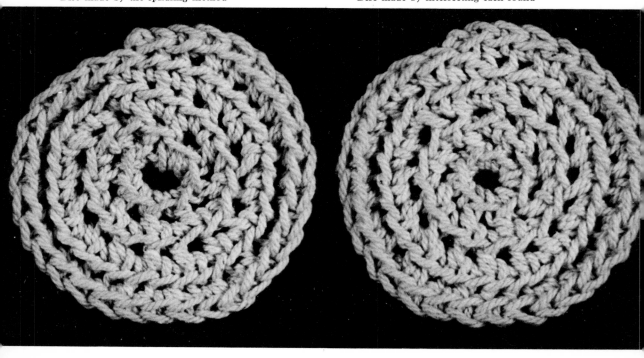

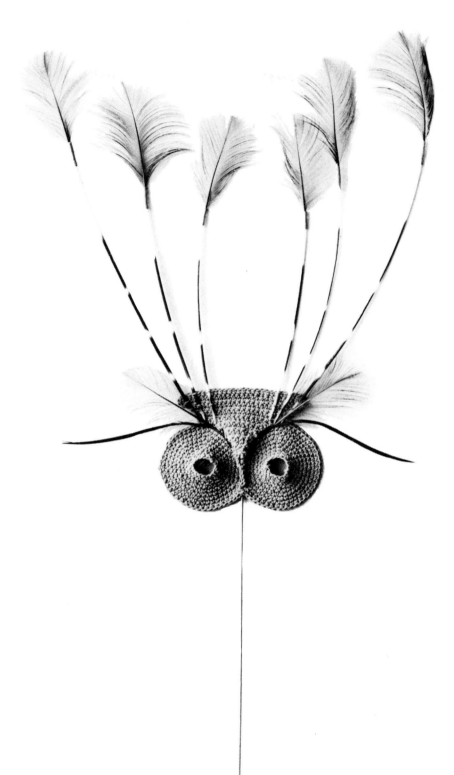

Mask, Terry Illes, polished India cord, porcupine quills, and feathers. Collection Dr. Roy Sieber. Even simple geometrical forms can be inventively and elegantly used. (Photo by David Repp)

The basic steps for all of the geometric shapes will be given in one manner only, but altering them or reversing them will often create new shapes, offering more possibilities to choose from. For example, a situation may arise that calls for making a disc or square from the perimeter inward toward the center. This can be done simply by reversing the directions given for making it from the center out.

In some cases the mirror image or opposite form can be made by reversing the directions. The triangle made first in the order suggested and then reversed will make a flat diamond shape. Using the same approach, the dome becomes a full sphere. Experimentation will show that many other shapes are possible.

Working in rounds

When making geometric shapes or forms, it is helpful to use a marker to keep track of each row or round of stitches. This is especially helpful with discs or tubular shapes to identify the point at which a round is completed. A safety pin, a paper clip, or a piece of colored yarn tied into a stitch at the beginning is most commonly used. Commercially made markers are also available for this same purpose.

On projects worked continuously round and round, there are two ways of working successive rows. One method is to spiral, much like the technique of coiling in basketry, making no intersection of rows as you work around. Since there is no point of union, the transition between rounds is smooth. To end a round you must taper the edge by grading down the height of stitch. For example, if you are working with a single crochet, make a few slip stitches before ending, which will lessen the step and create a smoother finish. The main disadvantage of this approach is that the rows will be slightly tilted, a pattern that may become evident on small pieces or when high stitches are used.

The second approach to working

rounds is to make an intersection at both ends of each round. Using a slip stitch, join the last stitch of each round to the first stitch. To begin the next round, add the number of chains needed to bring the yarn to the proper height for the stitch you have chosen, as though you were turning (one chain for single crochet, two for a half-double crochet, three for double, etc.). The primary advantages of this approach are that all rounds remain level and flat and that you do not have to taper the edge to make a smooth finish. The main disadvantage is that it may leave a visible union or seam where rounds intersect, depending on the choice of materials and scale. Use whichever of the two methods is more suitable for your personal needs.

With all geometric shapes that have flat or relatively flat sides, such as the oval, the hexagon, and the square, increases are only made at the corners or, in the case of the oval, at the rounds. The flat sides are worked even.

Disc

To make a disc, begin by making three chain stitches. Insert the hook back into the first chain and make eight single crochets in the same stitch, which completes the first round (Fig. 11-1). Depending upon the size and rigidity of the materials you are working with, you may find it advantageous to slightly increase the size of the first loop into which the eight single crochets are made. At the completion of the first round you have the options of either spiraling or making an intersection as explained earlier. In either case, the second round is made by increasing. Make two single crochets in each of the eight single crochets constituting the first round, which will make a second round of sixteen stitches (Fig. 11-2). The third round is made by putting two single crochets in each of the sixteen stitches from the second round. This makes a third round of thirty-two single crochets in the form of a disc.

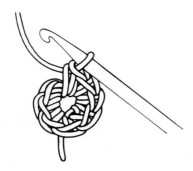

11-1. First round of disc, completed

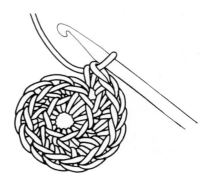

11-2. Second round of disc

From this point on you must alternate one round of regular single crochets with each round of increases. Although the disc is begun by increasing in every stitch, gradually fewer increases are made to keep the disc flat. This varies with the relationship between the materials, the hook you have chosen, the tension applied, and the height of the stitches.

To determine the rate of increase, merely watch what happens to the disc as you make it. If the edge begins to ruffle, your rate of increase is too rapid and you should begin spacing the increases. If the edge remains flat, and the part you have made previously begins to gather or ruffle, your rate of increase is too slow, insufficient to keep the piece flat. The solution is to increase more often. Practice will tell you what to look for and how to change the rate of increase.

Pot, Norma Lavy, 12 x 15 inches, jute and tufted sisal. A basic dome has been used to create a rigid container form with surface embellishment that gives the effect of ceramic glaze.

Dome

A dome or hemisphere is basically made with the same steps used to make a disc, but it is shaped by deliberately altering the flatness of the surface. Begin by making a disc and make fewer increases in each round, so the edge or rim will begin to turn up and form a bowl or dome. Your personal needs will dictate the shape of the dome and the rate at which you raise the sides. A good approach is to make a sample to determine how rapidly or how slowly you want the rim to turn up.

Once you have made a dome, or hemisphere, it follows that you can make a complete sphere by joining two domes rim to rim. This can be done in one piece if you make a dome as suggested and repeat the directions in reverse once you have reached the maximum circumference of the first half sphere. If you want a symmetrical sphere, it is imperative that you keep accurate information on the number of stitches and rounds in the first dome, in order to make the second one match.

Oval

An oval shape can be made simply by starting with a chain of five or more stitches. The first round is worked on both sides of the foundation chain, up one side and down the other, making three crochets in one stitch to round the ends. Once this basic shape is started, work even on the sides and increase on the ends to keep the work flat.

Oval

Hexagon

Square

Hexagon

To make a six-sided, or hexagonal, piece is very much like making a disc. Begin by making three chain stitches. Insert the hook back into the first chain and make six single crochets in the same stitch. As in the disc, the second round is made by increasing in every stitch. However, beginning with the third round, increase in every other stitch, and in the fourth round increase in every third stitch, and then in every fourth stitch, and so on. In each successive round, skip one more stitch. This is, in effect, increasing one stitch in each group of stitches divisible by six in that particular round. The increases create the angled corners of the six-sided piece; the double stitches always fall at the corners.

Square

To make a square, begin with three chains. Insert the hook back into the first chain and make eight single crochets in the same stitch, which completes the first round. Begin the second round by making one single crochet in the first stitch of the previous round. In the second stitch, make a triple stitch (three single crochets). Repeat this sequence a total of four times (Fig. 11-3). Each of the four triple stitches will subsequently become the corners of the square. The separate single crochets become the sides.

Start the third round by making a single crochet in the next stitch. In the triple stitch of the previous round, make a single crochet in the first stitch, a triple stitch in the center, and a single crochet in the third (Fig. 11-4). Repeat this sequence a total of four times to complete the third round.

With the completion of the third round you have made four corners (the triple stitches) with three single crochets between them that become the sides. In each successive round, the new triple stitches are placed in the center single crochet of the triple stitch of the previous round. These are spaced with single crochets. The sides will consequently be increased by two stitches each round. There will be five single crochets in the sides of the fourth round, seven in the fifth, etc.

When finishing off a square, complete the fourth corner, and then taper the edge with slip stitches to end off smoothly.

Obviously, a square can also be made from a succession of rows: you crochet back and forth with straight rows until the dimensions at the sides equal the length of the rows.

Cube

A cube can be made by extending the directions for a square. Make a square, and when you want to begin the sides, keep the number of stitches the same, and continue crocheting around the edges. The stitches will begin stacking up on one another and building a side wall that is exactly the same size as the perimeter of the square. When the height of the cube is reached, make a square for the top by reversing the directions for the bottom. Decrease three stitches into one at the corners as you make each successive round, thus enclosing the top of the cube.

You may find it helpful to make a round of slip stitches as you make the change from the flat bottom to the side wall and again from the side walls to the flat top. The slip stitches tend to make a firmer edge and a squarer turn.

11-3. Second round of square, completed

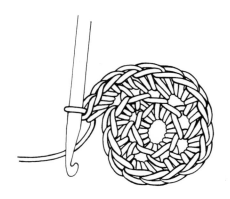

11-4. Third round of square, first sequence

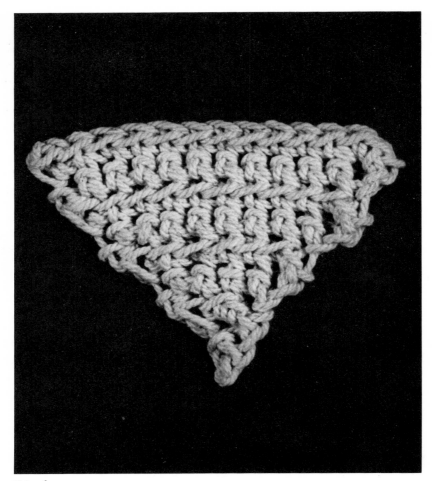

Triangle

11-5. First row of triangle

Triangle

A triangle is made by starting from one stitch and increasing in each successive row. The rate at which you increase will determine the shape of the triangle.

Begin by making two chains. Insert the hook back into the first chain and make a single crochet. Add one chain and turn. In the one single crochet, make three single crochets (Fig. 11-5). Add one chain and turn. Beginning with the third row, increase only at the ends of the row by putting two stitches in the first and last stitches. The third row consists of two stitches in the first stitch of the previous row, one in the second, and two in the

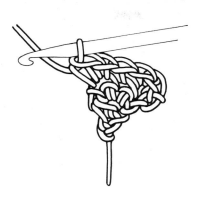

11-6. Second row of triangle

Ring. To show the ring more clearly a second round of single crochet has been added to the basic chain.

third (Fig. 11-6). Continue with these same basic steps, increasing at the outer edges until you have completed the triangle.

To make a more pointed triangle, that is, a triangle that is not equilateral, increase at one edge only. Beginning with the third row, put a double stitch in the last stitch of the previous row only.

If you have chosen fine yarns, both methods will leave small holes at the edge of the fabric. If this is an undesirable characteristic, it is possible to make the increases internally, toward the center of each row of stitches.

To make a flat diamond shape, first make a triangle and then reverse the directions when you have reached the maximum width, decreasing back down to a point.

Ring

A ring is made by simply joining both ends of a chain. Make a chain and insert the hook back into the very first stitch (Fig. 11-7), taking care not to twist the chain. Join the first and last stitches with a slip stitch (Fig. 11-8). The ring is complete, but you can continue working around the chain to make a broader band.

11-7. Joining a chain to make a ring, step one

11-8. Ring, step two

Cylinder. The surface texturing is achieved by reversing the direction of the crochet.

Curved tube with ends that are parallel, made by increasing on half of the tube and decreasing on the opposite side, is like a child's "slinky" toy with the top pushed to one side.

Cylinder

A cylinder or tube is made by starting from a ring. Continue to crochet around the ring without increasing or decreasing the number of stitches. The wall of a tube is made when the stitches begin stacking up on one another. As in making a disc, you have the choice of joining each successive round of stitches or spiraling to create the tube. If you choose to use the spiraling approach, you must end off by tapering the edge to avoid a step effect.

You can make a tube with the ribs on the outside or the inside, simply by reversing the direction in which you are working. To change the surface, work the height of the stitches down to a slip stitch, turn around and crochet in the opposite direction. This brings the ribs to the reverse side of the fabric.

By arbitrarily increasing or decreasing the number of stitches as you build the wall of the tube, you can make a very irregular shape. It is possible to make bulbous shapes by evenly increasing the number of stitches and then reducing them again. Here again, experimentation will disclose many possibilities.

There are three ways to make a curved tube—by physically bending a straight tube, thereby collapsing one side, and by crocheting a tube with a curved shape, in two ways described below. To curve a tube and make the bottom and top openings parallel to one another, increase one half of the tube and decrease the same number of stitches on the opposite side.

Curved tube with the ends not parallel, made by using a long stitch on one side and a short stitch on the other, is like a "slinky" toy with the top lifted at one side.

Free-form shapes and bulbous swellings can be made by randomly increasing, decreasing, and joining. Detail by Gayle Wimmer.

This will continue to give you a tube of the same diameter, but the tube itself will be displaced toward the side on which you increase.

To curve a tube and make the top and bottom openings not parallel—this makes an elbow bend or a right angle—make a short stitch on one side of the tube and a long one on the opposite side. For example, if you use a slip stitch on one side of the tube and a single crochet on the other, the tube will curve because one side is shortened. Combining both methods of curving a tube is also possible.

Many free-form shapes can be made by starting from one of the basic shapes described and randomly changing directions, making openings, joining pieces, crocheting off into space and back again.

12. ARMATURES AND STUFFING

The use of armatures presents many possibilities for structural support to the crocheter. At any given point an armature can be added to the piece. It can become a deliberate part of the exterior design or may be disguised so it is completely unobtrusive. Consider the armature's visual role, including its visual flexibility, and its structural role. If you want the armature to dominate, be bold about it and plan for the effect beforehand; if you want it to be subtle, choose an armature like the materials you are working with or cover it with the same materials.

Wall hanging, Lori Griffith, 72 x 20 inches, jute, horsehair, and satin cord. This sculptural hanging uses compound forms that have been joined and stuffed.

Helluvahooka, Clinton D. MacKenzie, wool, 32 x 18 inches in diameter. A freestanding form can be created by using an internal support, in this case a single rod rising from a flat base.

You can obtain materials to use for armatures and reinforcements in many places, such as a variety store for plastic or foam forms, a surplus store for paper- or cloth-covered wire, the Salvation Army for lampshade rings, or your local welding shop for large rings or forms. Look around you, and you may be surprised at what is nearby and suitable.

You can begin a piece from an armature by crocheting directly around the armature. Begin by drawing a slip knot onto the hook. Pass the yarn over the top rim of the armature and pass the hook under the armature. As though you have inserted the hook into a stitch, catch the yarn and draw it around the armature to the top and complete a slip stitch or a single crochet (Fig. 12-1). This then wraps the armature and makes an edge from which you can begin to crochet (Fig. 12-2).

If the armature comes as an afterthought, there are a few ways in which it can be included in the crochet. Try first to crochet around the armature, making it a structural part of the piece. If this does not work, wrap the armature and sew it to the back or inside of the piece unless such a procedure interferes with your aesthetic concept.

Another way to include an armature is to make a pocket hem into which a framework, rod, or wire can be inserted. This can be done on a flat fabric by extending the construction or, after finishing, by adding a band wide enough to

12-1. Single crochet around armature

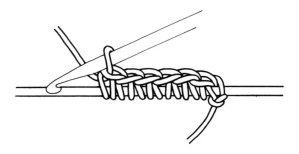

12-2. Single crocheted edge around armature

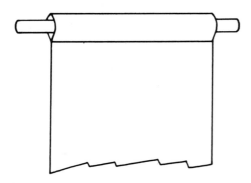

12-3. Simple pocket hem on a flat fabric

enclose an armature. The band will then be turned and joined together using one of the joining stitches or sewn so that it makes a pocket (Fig. 12-3).

To make a pocket hem on a circular piece, gradually increase or decrease to the midpoint of the pocket and then reverse directions back to the original number of stitches. This makes a shaped pocket for the armature. If you want the pocket to be part of the exterior finish, first increase and then decrease, making the hem larger than the piece. If you want to make it part of the interior structure, decrease first to the midpoint and then increase, making the hem smaller than the piece and therefore an

internal support. The rate of increase or decrease will vary, depending on the width of the band and the diameter of the circular piece.

Any of the closed-form crocheted pieces can be stuffed to fill out their shape. The nature of the stitch used in making the piece will determine whether you can stuff it directly or whether you will need a lining to prevent the stuffing from showing. There are many suitable materials for stuffing pieces, such as rags, shredded foam, polyester sheeting, polyester or cotton batting, and plastic foam pellets. One of the primary considerations for the selection of stuffing materials is the pliability and smoothness of the surface of the crochet. If it is slick or the fabric is very pliable, whatever stuffing material you choose will show. For a smooth surface use soft stuffing such as polyester.

If you are working with a fairly nonflexible fabric or coarse-surfaced material, there will be fewer problems to solve in stuffing, allowing you a broader selection of possible stuffing materials.

Other workable solutions to reinforcing forms include the use of rods to support collapsible forms as posts are used in a tent. Crochet forms also can be laid over skeletons of screening material or facing fabrics. Both these methods give an internal support without denying the crochet its soft character.

13. AFGHAN CROCHET AND HAIRPIN LACE

There are two types of crochet that are distinct from the rest in the way they are made. Afghan, or tunisian, crochet is made on an unusual hook, and hairpin crochet, or hairpin lace, is made on a frame.

Simple afghan crochet

Afghan crochet is used primarily for flat work and its design has a very obvious back and front. The throw we call an "afghan" took its name from the stitch. There are two basic afghan stitches that are technically similar but quite different in appearance: the simple afghan, which

is most common, and the knitted afghan, which has a knitted appearance. All afghan stitches are made in two parts on a long afghan hook. As in knitting, a complete row of stitches is picked up and retained on the hook and then each stitch is worked back off. There is in effect a "pick-up" row and a "stitch" row.

The simple afghan stitch is begun by making the usual foundation chain. To make the first stitch of the pick-up row, insert the hook into the second chain from the hook, catch the yarn, and draw a loop onto the hook. Continue this simple motion with each of the chains

Simple afghan crochet

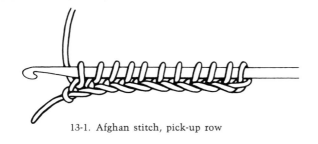

13-1. Afghan stitch, pick-up row

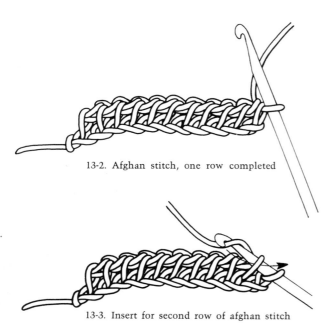

13-2. Afghan stitch, one row completed

13-3. Insert for second row of afghan stitch

on the foundation, retaining all the loops (Fig. 13-1).

When you have completed the pick-up row and are ready to begin the stitch row, catch the yarn and draw through one loop only. Next, catch the yarn and draw it through each pair of loops until you have completed all the stitches and only one loop remains on the hook (Fig. 13-2).

The second row of simple afghan stitches is begun by inserting the hook under the second vertical stitch element (the first is actually the right edge) of the previous row (Fig. 13-3). Catch the yarn and draw a loop onto the hook. Continue using the vertical element as though it were the chain referred to in the first row. Pick up each stitch and retain all the loops on the hook.

The stitch part of the second row is completed with the same steps as the stitch part of the first row.

Knitted afghan stitch

The knitted afghan stitch is started from one complete row of simple afghan stitches.

Knitted afghan crochet

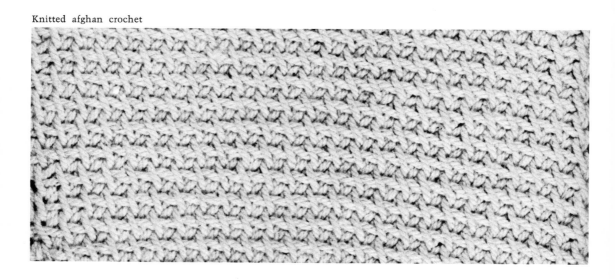

To begin the second row, insert the hook under the second vertical element and the top horizontal element (Fig. 13-4). Catch the yarn and draw it through onto the hook. Continue this step for the whole pick-up row. This is different from the simple afghan stitch in that two threads are picked up to begin each stitch, rather than one.

The stitch row is completed as in the simple afghan. However, this stitch row has a knitted look and a slightly more compact fabric body.

With afghan stitches you cannot work in the round. You can only work flat, and if you want to build three-dimensional shapes, you have to do it by joining. You cannot work randomly or freely as with regular crochet.

It is possible to increase and decrease in afghan stitching. To increase, wrap the hook once before inserting it into the stitch. This will give you an additional loop to draw through on your return, thus increasing by one stitch. To decrease, merely draw a loop directly through each three-loop group as you make the stitch row, instead of through each pair of loops.

Hairpin crochet

Hairpin crochet is made on a frame that traditionally resembled a fancy hairpin. The loom, known as a hairpin loom, is usually a U-shaped frame with a removable sliding bar that braces the two sides of the frame. The bar is taken off to remove stitches from the loom. A hairpin frame can be bought commercially in many different sizes and is easily made by bending a heavy wire or coat hanger into a U shape and then improvising a bracket across the open end to prevent the loops from slipping off.

Hairpin crochet is made in bands which are later joined together to make a loose and often lacelike fabric. The width of the work depends on the width of the hairpin loom or frame.

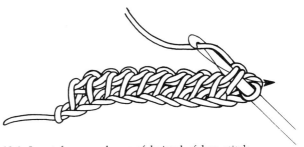

13-4. Insert for second row of knitted afghan stitch

Single band of hairpin crochet

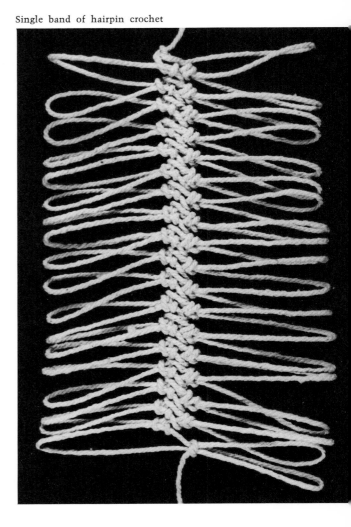

119

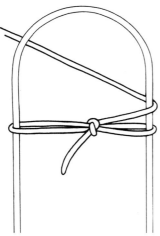

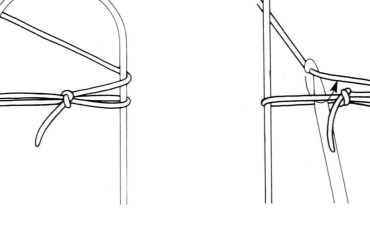

13-5. Wrapping the hairpin loom

13-6. Inserting under the front of the left loop of hairpin loom

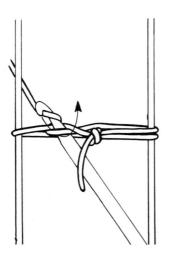

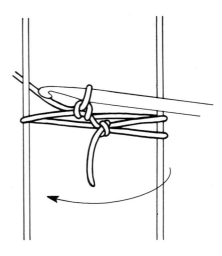

13-7. Drawing yarn onto hook in hairpin stitch

13-8. Hairpin stitch, completed. Arrow shows direction the loom turns for the second hairpin stitch

With the brace at the bottom, begin by wrapping the yarn around the hairpin loom and tying it so the knot comes in the center of the frame and joins both sides of the loop around it (Fig. 13-5). Pass the yarn around the right side to the back of the loom. Insert the hook under the front of the left loop (Fig. 13-6). Catch the yarn and draw it under the loop and onto the hook (Fig. 13-7). Reaching over the left loop, catch the yarn again and draw it through the loop on the hook, which completes the first hairpin stitch (Fig. 13-8).

Since each successive stitch is made on the opposite side of the frame from the previous stitch, you must either invert the hook or withdraw it from the loop after each stitch. If the frame is large enough, you can invert the hook by bringing the handle up toward the top and through to the other side. If the frame is small, you will have to remove the hook from the loop.

Next, turn the frame around so the right side comes forward and ends up on the left. If you have withdrawn the hook, reinsert it at this point. This brings the yarn around the right side of the frame to the back. Insert the hook under the front of the left loop, catch the yarn and draw it through onto the hook. Catch the yarn again and draw it through both loops on the hook, completing the second hairpin stitch (Fig. 13-9).

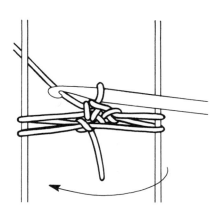

13-9. Second hairpin stitch, completed

Continue these steps, making each stitch on the opposite side of the frame from the one before. If the loom gets crowded, you may remove the bottom bracket and slide off all but a few stitches to continue working from.

There are several ways to join bands of hairpin crochet. One method is to lay two bands side-by-side and interloop them. Pick up one loop from the band on the right and draw it through a loop from the band on the left. Then draw a loop from the band on the left through the one you've brought from the right. Continue alternating from side to side, interlooping the respective bands. When the last pair of loops has been reached, they can be joined by stitching them together with a fine thread. One way of varying the design with this method of joining is to twist each loop before passing it through the next loop.

There are also many ways of crocheting bands of hairpin crochet together. The simplest is to join pairs of loops with a slip stitch. Begin by drawing a slip knot onto the hook. Twist a loop from the left band and insert the hook through it.

Two bands of hairpin crochet joined with a slip stitch, shown from the front

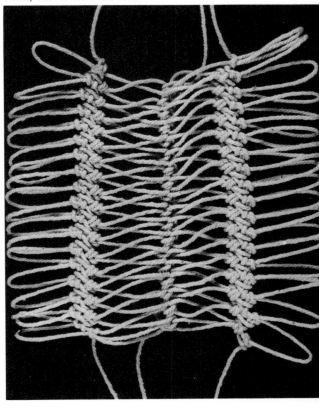

Twist a loop from the right band and insert the hook (Fig. 13-10). Next, join both loops together with a slip stitch, drawing through all three loops directly (Fig. 13-11). Continue picking up pairs of loops, one from each side, until you have completed joining the two bands.

A method of joining that makes a zigzag between bands is to loop from alternating sides with a chain stitch between. Draw a slip knot onto the hook, twist a loop from the left side, and insert the hook through it. Catch the yarn and draw through both loops. Add a chain. Twist a loop from the right side and insert the hook through it. Catch the yarn and draw through both loops. Add a chain. Continue this way, picking up a loop from alternating sides, until you have completed joining the bands. In addition to these methods, there are other fancy ways of joining bands that you may discover for yourself by experimenting.

There are also many techniques for finishing off the outside edges of hairpin crochet. The simplest is to join each loop to the next with a single crochet. If, however, you chose to pick up the loops alternately (or use any other fancy union), you may need to lengthen the outside edge so that the edge and the joining are the same length. To do this, insert one or more chain stitches between single crochets. Finishing the edges can be done in a number of ways that you should try on your own.

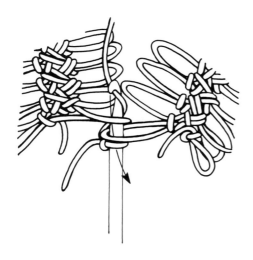

13-10. Joining bands of hairpin crochet with a slip stitch, step one

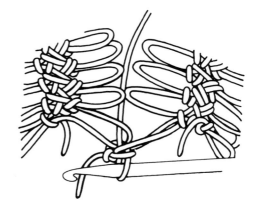

13-11. First joining stitch completed

122

14. CONTEMPORARY CROCHET

Crochet gives form, structure, mass, scale, and meaning to thread. It is a simple process, but it is flexible enough to produce a work of art when the construction follows basic aesthetic concepts. With crochet you can write your own story line, and make your fantasies grow from toys to monuments.

Crochet is among many techniques employed in recent art exhibits featuring non-loomed textiles. These exhibitions have proved that fiber forms are as integral a part of contemporary art as metal, wood, or plastic forms. Crochet is finding its way into wall hangings, body adornments, and soft sculptures. Whether the maker of a piece was looking for a process or the crocheter was looking for a form is incidental to the fact that a meeting of artistic traditions has taken place.

We are in a day and time when traditional boundaries in the arts are diminishing, and we have discovered that the textile craftsman is in the same league as the sculptor or painter. Of the artists working in fiber forms, many were originally textile designers who are now expressing themselves in new, free forms. Others are sculptors, painters, and designers applying the technique of crochet. The exchange that is taking place between these groups is creating a broader understanding and aesthetic through exposure to all forms of art.

With the exception of some crochet being in done in Eastern Europe, most of the exploration of new directions in crochet is taking place in America. Our lack of tradition, commonly thought of as a handicap, has freed us to try something that others may have been convinced couldn't be done.

The artist's spirit and his will to experiment makes all the difference in this new approach to an old craft. Crochet is essentially unlimited in its potential because it is open-ended in all directions, but sometimes we have to stick with it, push it, and exploit it in order to make it grow beyond the traditional boundaries. Scale in crochet is a matter of how much energy the artist is willing to expend.

Historically, crochet began as an art form, and now we are bringing it back to an art form. This evolution has been influenced by many factors, the single most important one being the contemporary artist, who is willing to turn to whatever process he needs to make his art. There has been a great deal of experimentation recently with all of the basic fabric construction techniques. The simplicity of translating concepts into fabric while using just one thread has given crochet its place in the new fabric arts. The hook is the crocheters pen, and with it he writes one line at a time to make his ideas come to life. This quality of working directly with the finished piece allows him to feel his way, making the crochet lacy or solid, soft or rigid.

The current movement emphasizes three-dimensional forms, or fiber sculp-

A Ribald (Fancy), Clinton D. MacKenzie, 102 x 22 inches in diameter. Collection of Jerome S. Sloan. Contrasting natural materials, metallic yarn, and a flocked ball, as well as a simple tubular construction pushed to its limits, creates the unusual sense of proportion that makes this piece a study in irony.

ture, and consequently a need has arisen for simpler approaches to making three-dimensional forms. Unlike woven forms, crochet can be conceived in and worked directly in three dimensions. It can be composed in one piece and, like pottery and glassblowing, can be fluidly molded in the making.

Basket Form, Clinton D. MacKenzie, 10 x 8 inches in diameter, natural raffia. The unique properties of raffia give rigidity to the form and an unusual irregular texture to the surface.

With crochet you can work fast enough to make a piece on a small scale (or one with large materials) in a single day. Such speed relieves the typical anxieties created by the more slow-moving fabric construction techniques. The spontaneity that crochet affords—the ability to rework and change pieces, to make corrections and to improvise—has contributed to its success. It is also a process that can easily be incorporated into other textile techniques. Crochet can literally be added to any other fabric and combined with many nonfabrics as well.

We are in the midst of a "back to the earth" movement, a make-your-own-things way of living, which has caused a resurgence of the handcrafts, including crochet, macramé, stitchery, and weaving. Especially with crochet there is a built-in requirement to design and craft your own work. Each piece is a new experience because there are so few limitations. There are no ends to premeasure, no grid set up, no framework of any kind. Few art forms offer so many seemingly opposite options: preplan or not, sketch or let it grow, draw a complete cartoon or be spontaneous, exercise control or freedom . . . make it your way. You feel freer to select a broader spectrum of concepts because there are no complicated mechanisms to employ that can come between you and the execution. Since you are alone with crochet, your work takes on a personal identity.

Until now, crochet has enjoyed a very limited exposure. The finished pieces shown in this last chapter represent the beginnings of crochet as an art form, and each has been selected for its interesting concept or special construction approach. Many of the works are student pieces because students tend not to be inhibited by preconcieved notions of what can or cannot be made. They just make it.

I hope you will be inspired to make a work of art. If not, I hope you will have gained a sense of appreciation for the exciting potentials of crochet.

Wall hanging, Caroline Potter, 9½ feet x 34 x 7 inches, black nylon, horsehair, wool. Weaving and crochet can be combined very effectively—here the crochet makes an additional layer of fabric, for trim, and tubes that spill out of the top. (Photo by Tim Brehm)

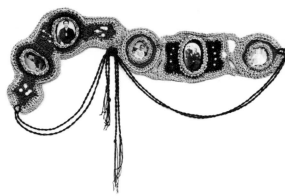

Floor sculpture, Sherry Cook, wool, 10 x 5 x 3 feet. Striped tubes are joined together and stuffed with unspun wool. (Photo by Robert Burningham)

Family Reunion, Jan Broderson, 6 x 36 inches, crocheted cord and tintypes. A nostalgic, mixed-media effect is created by framing old photographs with crochet, and then linking them together as a belt.

Soft sculpture, Ron Goodman, 10 feet by 24 inches. By extending the tubular structure and flow of free-hanging yarns, the artist entices the viewer to follow his sculpture in its movement through space. (Photo by Ron Goodman)

Fantasy animal, Linda Johnston, 30 x 10 inches, linen. The spiny animal is made of jagged shapes added to a central tubular form. (Photo by Robert Burningham)

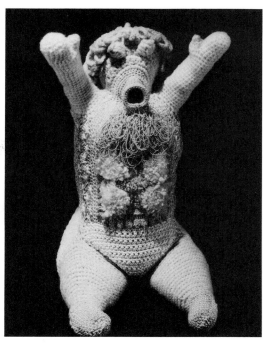

Soft toy, Linda Valeri, 10 x 24 inches, wool. Soft toys can be made by crocheting wool knitting yarns into simple forms.

Surrogate Baby, Del Feldman, 15½ x 7 inches, wool, acrylic, cord, raffia, rayon and taffeta ribbon, velour. (Photo by Malcolm Varon)

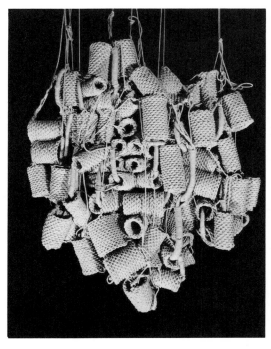

Soft sculpture, Carolyn Potter, 30 x 50 x 14 inches, jute and cheescloth. The loop stitch is used to make a shag surface on this crocheted stuffed form. (Photo by Tim Brehm)

Hanging sculpture, Naoko Furue, 36 x 36 x 6 inches, cotton seine twine. Simple cylinders are joined to make an effective sculpture. (Photo by Naoko Furue)

Shrine, Walter Nottingham, 4 x 2½ x 1 feet, wool, rayon, jute. Using wool, beads, and feathers, the artist builds a form that is crocheted, wrapped, and stitched. (Photo by Jack Lenor Larsen Studio)

Maine Form, Walter Nottingham, 84 x 36 inches, wool and rayon. This organic, gnarled form uses a large ring for an armature. (Photo by Robert Burningham)

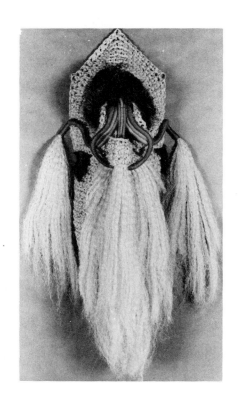

Wall sculpture, Lori Griffith, 60 x 36 inches, sisal, fur, wool. As well as creating unusual surfaces, stiff materials can be combined to provide relief structure for a crocheted piece.

Mask, Erica Wolfe, 18 x 14 x 12 inches, sisal. Three triangular planes are supplemented by stitchery to form a realistic animal mask.

Face Covering, Karen Vanderpool, 20 x 18 x 15 inches, linen and silver gimp thread. The attachments are made of tin cones and horsehair.

Mask, Nancy Woodward, 14 x 10 x 8 inches, jute. Each of the components was fabricated separately and then joined together.

Mask I, Clinton D. MacKenzie, 12 x 60 inches, wool. This is made on a circular armature in two layers, using only single crochet.

129

Full coat, Jan Broderson, wool. Unique and stylish garments can be created without the aid of a commercial pattern. (Photo by Howard Unger)

Body ornament, Bonnie Vierthaler. Very fine yarns are loosely crocheted into a lacelike fabric.

Haddies Heaven, Jan Broderson, 6 x 6 feet, wool. Organically dyed yarns were used to make a blanket that can equally well serve as an art fabric. (Photo by Howard Unger)

Stool, Janet Luks, 24 x 12 inches in diameter, crocheted wool, applique and rya techniques. Soft crater forms bring an added dimension to this rya stool. (Photo by Jeffrey Lewman)

130

Floor sculpture, Robert Mills, 9 x 6 x 3 feet, polyethylene tape stuffed with sheets of Saran. These synthetic materials give a shiny reflective surface to the whole piece. (Photo by Robert Mills)

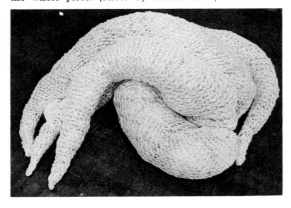

Oden's Shrine, Ursula Reeves, 24 x 24 inches, jute. This humorous piece is made of single crochet in tubes and discs, and then stuffed.

Soft tea set, Lori Griffith, 12 x 12 inches (teapot), cotton and jute twine. Pop art (or pot art?) in a satirical soft-sculpture group.

FOR LEFT-HANDED CROCHETERS

The left-handed crocheter often has difficulty getting started with crochet because most instructions are given for right-handed people. Directions and illustrations for making the chain stitch, single, double, and triple crochet are given here to help the left-hander through the initial steps.

Once a left-handed crocheter has begun to get the feel of crocheting, it will be easier for him to translate the typical right-handed directions. Visually, the mirror image of what the right-handed crocheter does is correct for the left-handed person. Perhaps a small hand mirror placed alongside of the illustrations in the other chapters of this book will help make them clear. The written directions need only be transposed from right to left and from left to right. The front to back instructions remain the same.

Since supplementary information about techniques is not included in this section, the left-handed crocheter must refer to

Chapter 4 for fuller instruction. Suggestions for easier manipulation of the stitches are given there.

Chain Stitch

If you are left-handed, hold nothing but the hook in your left hand. Hold the yarn and the body of the fabric in the right hand, so that your left hand is completely free to manipulate the hook. The right hand essentially remains still, the work being done with the left hand.

Begin by making a slip knot as described in Chapter 4. Insert the hook into the slip knot and draw the slip knot down onto the shank of the hook. You are now ready to begin crocheting. The chain stitch is the basic stitch that is compounded to make all other crochet stitches. To make the chain stitch, pass the hook to the right and under the yarn (Fig. A), catch the yarn and draw it through the loop on the hook, making a new loop or chain stitch. Repeat this

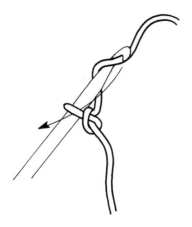

A. Chain stitch

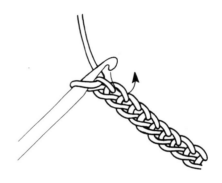

B. Insert for single crochet

stitch until the foundation chain is the desired length. Left-handed crocheters must always pick up the yarn by passing the hook to the right and under the yarn, unless otherwise directed.

Single Crochet

The left-handed crocheter should see the notes about non-ribbed and ribbed stitches in Chapter 4 before beginning the single crochet. The following steps are for the non-ribbed or regular single crochet.

Begin with a foundation chain of the desired length. Working from the front of the chain, start by inserting the hook from the front to the back into the *second chain* from the hook (Fig. B). The seeming extra stitch will give you the proper height at the edge of your piece. Catch the yarn by passing the hook to right of the yarn and under and draw it through the chain stitch and onto the hook (Fig. C), which leaves two loops on the hook.

C. Single crochet, step one

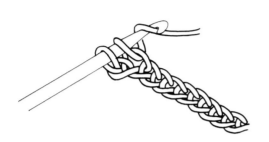

D. Single crochet, step two

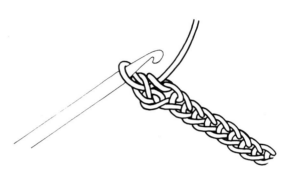

E. Single crochet, completed

Catch the yarn again and pull it through both loops (Fig. D). You have completed a single crochet stitch (Fig. E). Insert the hook into the next chain stitch and repeat the instructions until you have completed the first row of single crochets.

Double Crochet

Double crochet is a stitch that is two rows high and made in a single passage. It is also started from a foundation chain. Begin the double crochet by wrapping the yarn around the hook once (passing the hook from the right and under) and inserting it from the front into the *fourth chain stitch* from the hook (Fig. F). Catch the yarn and draw it through the chain onto the hook (Fig G), which will leave three loops on the hook. Catch the yarn and draw it through the first two loops on the hook (Fig. H). Catch the yarn again and draw it through the two remaining loops (Fig. I) to complete one double crochet (Fig. J). Repeat these steps in each of the remaining chains.

F. Insert for double crochet

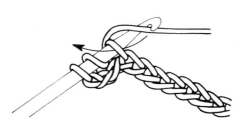

G. Double crochet, step one

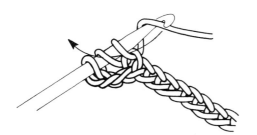

H. Double crochet, step two

I. Double crochet, step three

J. Double crochet, completed

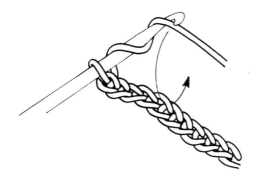

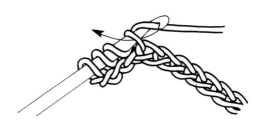

K. Insert for triple crochet

L. Triple crochet, step one

Triple Crochet

Triple crochet is started from a foundation chain with steps similar to those used for double crochet, and makes a stitch three rows high in one passage. Begin by wrapping the hook twice (passing the hook from the right and under) and inserting it from the front into the fifth chain from the hook (Fig. K). Catch the yarn and draw a loop through the chain and onto the hook (Fig. L), leaving four loops on the hook. Catch the yarn and draw it through two loops, three different times (Figs. M, N, O), to complete one triple crochet (Fig. P). Repeat these instructions for each of the remaining stitches on the foundation chain.

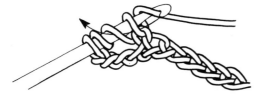

M. Triple crochet, step two

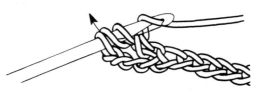

N. Triple crochet, step three

O. Triple crochet, step four

P. Triple crochet, completed

TABLES

Abbreviations commonly used in printed patterns

beg.....begin/beginning
bl.......block
ch.......chain
ch st....chain stitch
d c......double crochet
d ch....double chain
d cr.....double crochet
d tr.....double-triple crochet
dec......decrease
h dc....half-double crochet
half dc..half-double crochet
inc......increase
incl.....inclusive
l d......long double crochet
l tr......long triple crochet
o........over/yarn over
o m.....open mesh
p........picot
pr r.....previous row
r........row
rnd......round
s........same
s c......single crochet
s cr.....single crochet
s d c....short double crochet/
          half-double crochet
sk.......skip
sl.......slip
sl st.....slip stitch
st.......stitch
sts......stitches
tog......together
tr.......triple/treble
tr c.....triple crochet/treble crochet
tr ch....triple chain
tr tr.....triple-triple crochet/
          triple-treble crochet
w r h...wool round hook/yarn over
y o......yarn over

Additional explanations of printed patterns

The term "source yarn" refers to the yarn flowing from the source of supply.

Catching the yarn from the left and under is referred to as an "over," a "yarn over," or a "wool round hook."

When no increase or decrease is to be made, the term "work even" may be used.

When patterns are involved in making crochet, the directions may begin with the term "in multiples of," which actually means that you must be able to divide the total number of stitches by the number given. Multiples of 5, would be 5, 10, 15, 20, etc.

Occasionally a pattern will say "in multiples of +." Multiples of 5 + 3 would be 8, 13 (10 + 3), 18 (15 + 3), 23 (20 + 3), etc.

Asterisks (*) used in crochet directions mean to repeat the directions from the first asterisk to the last. If multiple asterisks are used (** or ***), it is generally because there are many sets of repeats within one set of directions. For example: Begin row 2—*2 dc in next st, sk 1 st, 1 dc in next * 6 times. Ch 1 to turn. Row 3—dec 1 st** 2 dc in next, dec 2 st ** 6 times. Ch 2 to turn. Row 4—***2 dc in next st, sk 1 st, 1 dc in next *** 6 times.

Parentheses or brackets most often mean the same thing as asterisks—to repeat the directions within.

Asterisks and brackets are usually accompanied by instructions to repeat the direction a specified number of times. A general rule of thumb is that asterisks with a number of repeats specified indicate that you should perform all operations up to the asterisk and *then* repeat them again the number of times specified. If parentheses are used, it usually means that you should include the first set of directions as part of the number of times indicated for repeating.

For example, "* 2 dc in next st, sk 1 st, 1 dc in next * 3 times" means to make two double crochets in the next stitch, skip one stitch, and make one double crochet in the next. Repeat these steps three times more for a total of four times. The same information given with brackets means repeat a total of three times: [2 dc in next st, sk 1 st, 1 dc in next] 3 times. This may vary with the particular set of instructions, so you must check the directions at the beginning of the source information.

A comparison between American and British names of stitches

AMERICAN	BRITISH
slip stitch	single crochet
single crochet . .	double crochet
half-double crochet	half-treble crochet
double crochet . .	treble crochet
triple crochet . . .	double-treble crochet
double-triple crochet	triple-treble crochet
triple-triple crochet	quadruple-treble crochet
long triple	long treble

A comparison among hooks of various materials and sizes

Steel	14-4	3	2	1	0	00										
Aluminum			B		C	D	E	F	G		H	I	J	K		
Plastic						D	E	F	G		H	I	J	K		
Plastic						3		4	5	6	7	8	9	10	10½	
*Afghan			B		C	D	E	F	G		H	I	J			
Bone (tapered)			1		2	3	4	5	6							
Wood											I		L	M	N	
Wood											10		11	13	15	16
Giant Plastic																Q S
diameter											¼"	5⁄16"	⅜"	7⁄16"	½" 5⁄8" ¾"

*Afghan hooks—numbers correspond to knitting needles of same letter.

CROCHET TERMS

English	French	Spanish
chain or chain stitch	maille chaînette	cadena
crochet	crochet	crochet or tejer con gancho

crochet hook	crochet
	  or aiguille de crochet
		gancho
		  or aguja de crochet

decrease	diminuer	menguados or diminuir puntos
double crochet	bride	macizo triple
increase	augmenter	aumentar
insert	piquer	pinchar or metirse
loop	boucle	hebilla, gaza, or lazada
repeat from*	reprendre a*	repetir desde* or volver a tomar*
row, previous row	rang, rang précédent	hilera, hilera anterior
single crochet	demi-bride	macizo doble
skip (as "skip a stitch")	sauter	saltar
slip stitch	maille glissée	punto deslizado
stitch	maille	punto, or macizo
triple crochet	double-bride	macizo cuádruple
yarn	fil	hilo

yarn over
  or wool round hook
	faire un jeté	hilo por encima
		  or lazada por encima

German	Italian
Kettenstich or Luftmasche	catenella or maglia volante
Häkelarbeit or häkeln	uncinetto or lavoro a crosché
Häkelnadel	uncinetto
abnehmen	diminuire
Stäbchen	maglia alta
aufnehmen or zunehmen	aumentare
einstechen or einsetzen	passare or entrare or puntare
Schlinge	asola
wiederhole von*	ripetere da*
Reihe, frühere Reihe	riga or giro, giro precedente
feste Masche	maglia bassa
auslassen	saltare
Masche überziehen	punto scorso or mezza maglia bassa
Stich or Masche	maglia or punto
Doppelstäbchen	maglia alta doppio
Garn or Faden	filo
1 Umschlag	fare un gettato

BIBLIOGRAPHY

Anchor Manual of Needlework. Boston: Charles T. Branford Co., 1958

Birrell, Verla. *Textile Arts: A Handbook of Fabric Structure and Design Processes.* New York: Harper College Books, 1959

De Dillmont, Therese. *Encyclopedia of Needlework, DMC Library.* New York: Joan Toggitt, Ltd.

Emery, Irene. *Primary Structures of Fabrics.* Washington, D.C.: Textile Museum, 1966

Lindsey, Ben. *Irish Lace: Its Origin and History.* Dublin: Hodges Figgis and Co., 1886

Maddox, Marguerite. *Complete Book of Knitting and Crocheting.* New York: Pocket Books, Inc., 1971

Mathieson, Elizabeth Laird. *The Complete Book of Crochet.* Cleveland: World Publishing, 1946

Peake, Miriam Morrison. *The Wise Handbook of Knitting and Crocheting.* New York: William H. Wise and Company, 1949

Thomas, Mary. *Mary Thomas's Knitting Book.* New York: Joan Toggitt, Ltd.

Von Krause, Fritz. *In Dem Wildnissen Brasiliens.* Leipzig: F. Voigtlander Verlag, 1911

INDEX